Traplines

Traplines

Coming Home to Sawtooth Valley

JOHN REMBER

Pantheon Books

New York

Traplines, originally titled *Memory Tricks*, is published by Pantheon Books by special arrangement with James R. Hepworth and Confluence Press, Lewis-Clark State College, 500 8th Avenue, Lewiston, Idaho 83501-2698.

Portions were originally published in slightly different form in the following: *Boise Magazine, Boise Weekly, Departures, The Idaho Mountain Express*, and *Snow Country Magazine*.

Library of Congress Cataloging-in-Publication Data

Rember, John.
Traplines : coming home to Sawtooth Valley / John Rember.
p.   cm.
ISBN 0-375-42207-2
1. Rember, John—Childhood and youth.
2. Authors, American—Homes and haunts—Idaho—Sawtooth Valley.
3. Rember, John—Homes and haunts—Idaho—Sawtooth Valley.
4. Sawtooth Valley (Idaho)—Social life and customs.
5. Authors, American—20th century—Biography.
6. Sawtooth Valley (Idaho)—Biography.   I. Title.

PS3568.E5574 Z475 2003
813'.54—dc21   2002035498
[B]

www.pantheonbooks.com

Book design by Robert C. Olsson

Printed in the United States of America

First Pantheon Edition

2 4 6 8 9 7 5 3 1

For my mother and father

Contents

Acknowledgments

Sections of this work have been published in *Snow Country Magazine*, *Travel and Leisure*, *Boise Magazine*, *Boise Weekly*, and *The Idaho Mountain Express*, and anthologized in the volumes *Written on Water*, *Where the Morning Light's Still Blue*, and *Father Nature*. I wish to thank Chris Farnsworth, Alan Minskoff, Pam Morris, and Kathleen Ring for their editing, encouragement and friendship, and Erik Henriksen for a perceptive and honest reading. Jim Hepworth's faith in my writing has kept me a writer when I might have tried my hand at creative accounting instead, and Dan Frank, as an editor and wonderfully intuitive reader, has shown me deep and quiet places in my stories where other stories lay hidden. Without the help of these people, and without the bright presence of Julie Rember in my life, this book would not have been written.

In the early spring of 1961 a friend and I were making a snow fort on Warm Springs Avenue in Ketchum, Idaho, when Ernest Hemingway walked up and began staring at us.

After a few minutes he said, "What are you doing?"

We replied that we were making a snow fort.

A little while after that he said, "Hello, boys."

We said hello.

"What are you doing?" he said again. We had already answered that question. He stared at us in silence for a while, and then hobbled on down the road.

It was the post-shock-therapy Hemingway. He was gaunt and crazed and looked a hundred years old. If he had been a phoenix, he would have been in flames.

My friend's father ran a welding shop, and the day Hemingway killed himself Mary Hemingway brought the shotgun into the shop and had it cut into little pieces with an electric hacksaw. She left with the pieces in a canvas bag.

I knew then that whatever else I might become, I would never become a writer.

A long time later I came to Hemingway as a writer, and my dealings with him can be summed up this way: every time I'm working on a story and I think I'm discovering a new technique or finessing an old one, I find that he did the same thing better long ago.

But I hope my intent is different. Hemingway's suicide has always stayed with me. I know that his work and his death are intertwined, but it's still a shock to pick up The Sun Also Rises *and see its hero, the imperfectly constructed Jake Barnes, end that book alone, impotent, defiant, in despair, and in love with death. In the end, Hemingway bagged the biggest, most dangerous story of them all as it charged at him from out of the concrete and Formica surfaces of his house in Ketchum.*

The stories in this book are fragments of my life and my memory and my imagination. I've tried to be kind to their truths, even when those truths aren't kind to me. I've also tried to keep my own perceptions from becoming the tools of the kill.

All our stories rest on other, older stories, and if we're careful, and if we're kind, and if we pay deep attention to memory and its tricks, we can bring forth our stories and keep those older stories intact. It's a way of saving our lives.

Traplines

Coming Home to Sawtooth Valley

I N 1987 I cashed out of the ski resort of Sun Valley, Idaho, and went fifty miles north to my family's place in Sawtooth Valley to build a house. I did so out of a deep homing instinct—the same forty acres that had sustained our tiny herd of horses every summer for thirty-five years had sustained, for me, a vision of a place where I belonged in the world, where I could get up in the morning, step out the door, and catch dinner from the Salmon River, or simply step out to watch the sunrise light the Sawtooths above their dark foothills. And then, depending on my horoscope in a week-old *Idaho Statesman* or the shape of the morning's clouds, I could fix the fences, cut firewood, change the water on the pasture, plant trees, or just fish some more.

It was a vision of a life, I think now, that came from memories of our horses, brought from winter pasture every June, whinnying and bucking around the fence lines, biting into the spring grass, running full-gallop through the shallow water on flooded river islands, home at last. Such memories become metaphors, and in early middle age, such metaphors become calls to action.

So when I found myself in the unexpected financial condition of being able to return home, I did. The house was begun in September 1988 and, owing to good weather all through that fall, was finished in February 1989.

That March I sat at my desk, warm and comfortable, the nearby cold of the Sawtooth Valley spring held harmless by thermopane windows and six inches of fiberglass. If I looked up from my monitor, I could see the cold stone towers of Mount Heyburn, their ragged edges smoothed by thick drifts of snow. The willows in the river bottom were skeletal and frosted, but every bit as beautiful as they would be that July, when the horses would hide in them to escape the flies and the heat. The snow on the valley floor held my weight in the mornings, and at least once a day I went out to wander the fence lines, or sat on the melted-off riverbank to watch the flyovers of returning geese, or skied the hill behind the house, or ran to the mailbox when I heard the mailman accelerate toward his next target, my neighbor's mailbox a mile up Highway 75. Home at last.

But it wasn't home. I found what once was familiar was unfamiliar. What once was real was no longer real. Everything might have looked the same to the horses that spring, but things had become more surface than substance for me.

That fall the power crew spent a few days digging trenches and driving a pipe under the highway in order to run power underground from the pole on the other side of the road to the house. There were to be no wires in the air outside the windows of my home.

The United States Forest Service wanted it that way. That agency is charged with maintaining the pastoral values of Sawtooth Valley as part of its larger mission of overseeing the Sawtooth National Recreation Area, a central Idaho enclave of fun that includes the Sawtooth, White Cloud, and Boulder Mountain Ranges, and the small patches of flat ground between them. Forest Service agents were authorized to purchase land and easements under the 1974 Act of Congress that established the SNRA, and while my family was lucky enough to be allowed to stay, the Forest Service has told us what structures we may build and where they may be placed ever since they bought the easement on our property. In their view, electrical wires and pastoral values do not mix, and so the wires went underground.

I wanted them underground anyway. A wire running into a house looks ugly, as do the strung-together lines of great steel crosses stretching across formerly pagan Idaho deserts. They remind me of the wires that run above any of western America's commercial strips: wires that power neon signs, the flash fryers of franchise restaurants, the spotlights of auto showrooms, and the hundreds of whirling ceiling fans hanging over home-care customers.

But as I was pulling underground cable along the bottom of the trench that led to my house, I remembered the summer of 1955, when I watched with a child's awe as the Rural Electrification Administration planted the first power poles in the glacial gravel of Sawtooth Valley. I was only five, but I can remember sensing the great expanding outside nation that those poles represented.

People outside the valley walls cared about us, we who lived in this most remote place, and were including us in their progress. No longer would we have to use oil lamps for illumination. No longer would our radios run off car batteries. No longer would we be people without power.

The only analogous experience I have had since is watching the ending of the film *Dr. Zhivago*. There, the final image of a great hydroelectric dam clears away messy images of human tragedy and replaces them with crystalline Soviet light. At age five, in wonder and delight, I switched the newly wired lights of our cabin on and off and on again. At age five, I would not have wanted to bury the power lines.

The next year, a substantial section of the highway between Sun Valley and Stanley was paved, including the section in front of our home.

My father was a fishing and hunting guide. The paved road meant more tourists, and more tourists meant better business. His clients would come to the house at four a.m. for sourdough pancakes and strong black coffee. After breakfast, he would take them back through the willows to the river, hook a Chinook salmon, and hand them the pole so they could land it, all for $10 per person per day. He didn't guarantee them a fish, just a fish on the line.

In the spring, before the salmon runs, my father and his clients would fish in the inlets of Redfish Lake for bulltrout, and I can remember days when a limit of trout, spread out on the grass of home for a photo opportunity, weighed more than a limit of salmon.

It was a kind of paradise we lived in. We had electricity, paved roads, a new '56 Ford, and an endless string of professional visitors—doctors, lawyers, CEOs, and politicians, all of them from places like New York and Dallas and Washington, D.C.—who assured us that we were living the kind of life they would live if they could only break free of their responsibilities to live it. I took literally every yearning word they spoke, even when the snow drove us out every fall and we moved south over Galena Summit to the Wood River Valley, where my mother was a nurse at the Sun Valley Hospital and my father drove ski bus after his fall trapping season ended. By Christmas, our southern freezer was full of venison and elk and the French-bread shapes of paper-wrapped salmon, and we had only to look at our dinner plates to know where we were based and where our sustenance lay. Every May we returned, over the still-frozen Galena, to a valley mirror-bright with water and new willow leaf, noisy with the sounds of nesting birds and the roar of rapids.

This world lasted longer than it had any right to. It lasted long enough for me to be raised in it. It lasted, I suppose, from our '56 Ford to our next car, a '65 Ford. But the power lines and the paved roads and the Fords and even the salmon in the river were destabilizing forces, and eventually it came to an end.

The valley became crowded with people. Some of our neighbors began subdividing their ranches and selling them off, taking the money and running to places that were warm in the winter, where life was neither as beautiful nor as hard as it was in Sawtooth Valley. They left behind them little deposits of summer cabins, where people from Twin Falls and Boise and Pocatello spent summer weekends. The sagebrush flat just west of Obsidian Mountain, three miles upriver from our place, came to be filled with trailers and prefabricated kit houses.

In the Salmon River there were fewer and fewer salmon. The Army Corps of Engineers, afflicted with the same naive fascination with power I had displayed at the light switch of our cabin, had built great roaring spillways on their hydroelectric dams on the Columbia and the Snake Rivers. Slack water and turbines killed millions of little salmon swimming to the oceans, and the depleted returning runs faced gill nets, nonfunctional fish ladders, and the nitrogen-poisoned waters flowing from the spillways.

Government programs poisoned grasshoppers with DDT in Sawtooth Valley, and we stopped seeing eagles and hawks and ospreys and herons. The Idaho Fish and Game Department used Toxaphene to poison Petit Lake, ten miles upriver from us, and inadvertently poisoned the river as far downriver as Stanley, baby salmon and all. Four years later, in August, my father rode up the river for three miles, looking for spawning salmon and didn't find a single one. By that time he had stopped guiding for a living and had begun working as a mechanic and welder for road construction projects.

By 1974 Sawtooth Valley had been cut up into thousands of pieces. Plans for condo projects on the moraine above Stanley had been drawn up and were about to be implemented. A good percentage of Castle Peak in the White Clouds was determined to be molybdenum, and ASARCO

—a mining company—was planning to build a road into it and carry it away, bit by profitable bit.

The act of Congress that established the Sawtooth National Recreation Area had the effect of reversing many of these later changes. In Sawtooth Valley, except within three small designated communities, parcels of land under twenty acres were purchased outright by the Forest Service. Larger parcels, such as our place, were placed under strict zoning to preserve the early-ranching character of the valley, and their owners were compensated for the difference between what the land was worth as agricultural land and what it was worth as homesites. In most cases, this represented about 95 percent of the land's value.

It was as if the valley was suddenly populated with lottery winners. One of our neighbors put his easement check into certificates of deposit and made more in interest that year than he had in his best year ever raising cows.

ASARCO was paid for molybdenum still in the ground. Castle Peak is intact, and no road has been built to its base. The Sawtooth Primitive Area became a wilderness, and mining claims within its expanded boundaries were disallowed. No longer could motorcyclists ride to the ridge above the north side of Sawtooth Lake. No longer could miners claim the beryllium deposits under Glen's Peak or the gold that lies far under Goat Creek, where it hits the South Fork of the Payette above the old Sawtooth Lodge at Grandjean.

And some salmon did come back. They were hatchery fish, barged down around the dams, and were distinguished from what are called wild fish by clipped fins. In that first August after my house was finished, I found dead salmon on gravel bars, spawned out, evidence—for anyone who needs it—that sex and death are connected. There weren't enough of them to re-create the stench of earlier spawning seasons, when you could smell dead salmon all up and down the river, but the people a mile downriver at the new Sawtooth fish hatchery insisted that they were working toward that end.

I tried not to count on it. I knew that the salmon in the Salmon River after the last Columbia dam had been built would have more in common with my neighbor's domestic cows than with the wild salmon I caught when I was ten and twelve. Raised in a hatchery, transported over dams on their way to the ocean and back from it, caught again and again by human handlers who were trying to get them back— almost—to my backyard, they had become artificial wildlife.

In the intervening years, every third fish has been allowed to swim on up the river from the hatchery, there to spawn under the gaze of tourists. The rest have been slit open and milked of their eggs and sperm. Fertilization has taken place in a bucket. Death, for them, has preceded sex.

It's illegal to fish for salmon above the hatchery, so I haven't seen salmon fishermen elbow to elbow on the river-banks behind my house. I haven't crept back through the willows with a salmon rig to catch the product of years of ex-pensive work by the salmon restoration industry. It wouldn't be catching a wild fish. It wouldn't even be poaching. It would be rustling.

There are still cows in the valley, but their owners worry more about the price of money than the price of beef. The ranches are still here, as pastoral as ever, but their owners are often elsewhere, especially during the coldest part of the winter. Some of the old ranch houses have been torn down and giant new log homes have been built for new owners, who live here during the summer and fall.

We have a population of caretakers. They're nice people and good neighbors, but they have trouble saying the words "my home." The people here who look most like cowboys wrangle dudes up and down the Sawtooth trails in the summer.

There has been talk for years of burying the power lines that run along Highway 75 and enhancing our pastoral values yet another degree. The electrical co-op we belong to doesn't think it's a good idea. The cold of the winters here would make it impossible to dig down to a frost-damaged line. But I hope they figure out a way to get around that problem, because like the landscape architects at SNRA headquarters, I think it would look better. The lines strung from power pole to power pole are a too-visible reminder of the power produced outside the valley walls, where acidic coal smoke and silt-ridden reservoirs and radioactive waste are the byproducts of the electricity that keeps this house bright at night. I'd prefer the connection to be hidden and the lights to go on as if by magic.

Should the lines ever be buried, Highway 75, now officially designated a scenic highway, will carry summer tourists through a valley that looks almost as it did in 1956. Salmon will be in the river below the hatchery. Ranchers who live on wide expanses of land will be running up and down the road in pickup trucks. Some of us who live here will be out digging ditch or fixing fence or working with horses. Perhaps a bit of pageantry will be detectable in our motions.

There are worse lives than those lived in museums. There are worse shortcomings than a lack of authenticity. Trouble with unreality is much preferable to trouble with reality. So I get up in the morning, open the doors to the sun and tree-cleaned air and a backyard river that has never known a discharge of treated effluent, look up at mountains that tear holes in the clouds, watch the eagle that has made this stretch of river his home this winter, and consider myself among the luckiest of men. But that's because this place that I live in now reminds me that once I had a home in Sawtooth Valley, when the fish were wild in the rivers, when our neighbors had always been cowboys, and when a flip of the switch brought wonderful, magical, incredible light.

Stanley

S TANLEY SITS in the midst of wildflower meadows under
Thompson and Williams and Goat Peaks, just above
where Valley Creek comes in from the west to join the waters of the Salmon. State Scenic Highways 75 and 21 inter-
sect there. Every point on Stanley's horizon is mountain or
forest. Its main street is 6,200 feet above sea level.

In the summer, Stanley's population is twenty times what
it is in mid-January. It has only 100 permanent year-round
residents, according to the signs on the roads leading into
town, but that total is nearly triple the thirty-six it had when
I started elementary school there in 1957. At that time, the
town consisted of six city blocks in two rows of three, di-
vided by Main Street, which held the eight-room Sawtooth
Hotel, the post office, a general store, the elementary school,
and four bars: the Rod and Gun Saloon, the Stanley Club,
the Ace of Diamonds, and John and Mary's. The school was

a two-room Quonset hut on Main Street. Grades one through four were in one room and grades five through eight were in the other. That fall, I was the only one in the first grade.

The surviving documents of my first-grade experience are a collection of crayoned pages and a report card. The report card, for the first ninety days of that fall, contained a single grade—S, for satisfactory—my first experience of the reduction of a substantial portion of my life down to a single evaluative mark.

Ten other students were in the lower-grade room with me. During the time that Mattie Hansen, the teacher, was occupied with the lessons for the second, third, and fourth grades, I was given crayons and a sheaf of blank pages. I remember being told to color, but most of my drawings are crude monochrome representations of cold, empty mountains and solitary pine trees, stick-elk and stick-horses, always in purple or black or brown.

When I did use a second color in a drawing, it was red, put there to represent blood. One faded, crumbling sheet is covered with my attempt to render my father sitting in the back room of the ranch house, flaying fur from flesh, a crude figure with a huge knife between two scribbled piles of dead animals. One pile is brown and covered with hundreds of small straight marks to represent fur. The other, even now, a half-century away, glistens to my Rorschach-trained eyes as red and as wet as lip gloss. Both piles have crude animal faces in them, and some of the faces have eyes, and some of the eyes gaze at me with interest across five decades.

The memories I have of that time at Stanley Elementary

School don't reflect as much pathology as my drawings. I remember the community dances we had in the other, larger room of the school, where people from all over the valley showed up to hear Phyllis Williams, the teacher for the four upper grades, play waltzes and marches on the school's old piano. I remember dancing the Varsouvienne with a beautiful dark eighth-grade girl, Jill Klopfenstein, and I remember that she had on moccasins and a turquoise dress with a silver-and-turquoise belt that scraped my cheek when I danced with her. I remember a community bingo game held in the smaller room, where I bingoed and won a pair of large yellow-and-black foam dice that were supposed to be hung from the rearview mirror of a car. I was excited that our car was going to have foam dice hanging from its rearview mirror, but my parents were inexplicably embarrassed by it and made me take it back to the prize table and exchange it for a pen-and-pencil set.

I remember recess, playing on the swings and being part of an ongoing game of Cowboys and Indians that was organized by the older students, who brought cap guns and fixed-blade hunting knives to school as fashion accessories. If you had a cap gun or a knife you could be either a Cowboy or an Indian, depending on your predilections or your ancestry, but if you didn't you had to be a horse, which mostly involved making whinnying noises and running around the schoolyard in a panic when the cap guns started going off.

When I went home after the first week and asked my parents for a cap gun of my own, my father said that he didn't ever want me thinking that a gun could be used for anything other than a tool to kill something. I could have a real gun, but not a cap gun, and after school he began teaching me to shoot in the backyard, firing a .22 caliber single-shot rifle at bottles balanced on fence posts. When I hit a bottle, my father would tell me, as a kind of ritual, never to point a gun at anything that I didn't want broken into little tiny pieces.

From the schoolroom itself I remember a forty-eight-star flag on the wall, the alphabet tacked below it, white block letters on dark green twelve-inch by twelve-inch cards. At the front of the room, above the window that looked out to the Sawtooths, was a picture of George Washington, who was introduced as the Father of Our Country. I remember Mattie Hansen hitting a boy named Harry Newcomb with a yardstick for reciting the Pledge of Allegiance while standing with his feet spread wide apart on the linoleum floor. Harry had been warned several times that this posture was unacceptable to the school and to George Washington and to the flag itself, and when the yardstick came down I remember thinking that if you were going to disobey the teacher, you should pay attention to who else was on her side. I had a desk in one corner, and I found that if I kept quiet and stared out the window at Williams Peak or scribbled away with crayons, Mattie would leave me in peace until it was time to go home and shoot bottles.

If there was a first-grade curriculum, I have no idea what it was. In November it got too cold to keep water in the pipes of our house, and we moved down and south to the Wood River Valley.

I continued my education at Ketchum Elementary School, where I found myself ninety days behind the thirty other first-graders. I couldn't read, and they could. I couldn't make letters and they could. In Ketchum, the coloring books all had drawings in black already done, and the task was to fill them with color, staying within the lines, but I couldn't do that either.

I remember the first-grade teacher in Ketchum holding up one of my attempts at making an alphabet and telling everyone that "John Rember's paper was the worst one in the class today." When she handed it back I tore it into shreds in front of her. She started to say something to me, but went silent and turned away and sat down at her desk and when she looked at me I saw she was about to cry. It was the first time I realized adults were people too, and it wasn't a happy realization.

After that I began making letters with the aid of an alphabet stencil that was in the middle of my ruler. It was tedious work, but my papers began to look enough like those of the other students that I was no longer singled out for abuse.

When I told my parents that I had to use a ruler to make my letters, they asked me if any of my classmates did the same. I said I was the only one and then we had a family conference. I have a vivid and happy memory of my mother telling me that I shouldn't feel bad if I wasn't the smartest one in the class. There are lots of other things you can do in life, she said, besides be good in school. Simply do the best you can, she said. It isn't necessary to do more.

I should say that the first-grade teacher who held me up to ridicule finally did teach me to read that year. She introduced me to arithmetic and showed me how green and gold and silver and blue could be brought into my black, purple, and red landscape. She showed us maps of the world and showed us how small we were in it. She cared deeply about her students, and after a rocky start, she gave me strengths—one of them the knowledge that I could endure small cruelties—that have served me well.

I wanted to return to second grade in Stanley the next fall, but as soon as the school year started, my mother took my brother and me to school in Wood River. My father ran his traplines into November and then joined us. We continued in this way through my elementary-school years.

Sawtooth Valley remained the center of our lives. In Ketchum and Sun Valley and Hailey we told people that we were from Stanley. It was a way of not having to use land-marks and mileposts to explain where we lived in Sawtooth Valley. Stanley was town for us, when we went to town.

Inside Sawtooth Valley, however, such talk was careless and violated important social distinctions. If we had really been from Stanley, we would have had to live within the city limits. We would have had to stay through the winter, and insulated houses in town rented at a premium. There was no work. There was no high school, which meant that my brother would have had to board in a dormitory in the town of Challis, fifty-five miles downriver. And even though Stanley could get at least one Boise TV station, the reception was complicated by the crystalline mutterings of the Sawtooths, which filled picture tubes with snow so thick you often couldn't tell Eisenhower from Khrushchev on the evening news.

People who did contribute to the official Stanley total of thirty-six endured all these things and worse. Winters in Stanley were hard to get through without fundamental changes in mood and outlook. By February, the previous summer's new friendships, community spirit, cooperative projects, and collective hopes for the future had usually fallen victim to an undifferentiated mixture of envy, boredom, sloth, avarice, and anger, manifested in paranoia, vicious gossip, and sheer joy at the misfortunes of others. About all the locals could agree on by March was that they had made it through another winter in excessive proximity to one another and that anyone who hadn't was an outsider and therefore doubly suspect.

So, inside Sawtooth Valley we were careful to point out that we lived ten miles upriver from town.

Evidence of
Grandmother

L ATE ONE NIGHT, a few years before she died, my
grandmother left her house in Hailey, Idaho, and
drove fifteen miles south. There she turned left off the highway and drove onto the rough dirt road that runs along the
Timmerman Hill ridgetop until she reached a small knoll.
She got out of the car and waited in the darkness until far to
the south she saw a quick high needle of red light. Then she
drove back to her house. She had witnessed the flash of an
above-ground atomic test in Nevada.

At the time I was too young for school. Both my parents
worked, and I stayed with my grandmother during the
weekdays. In the weeks after her trip to Timmerman Hill, I
was witness to the effect that watching the Bomb had had on
her. She read books on nuclear weapons and on the doomed,
prewar Hiroshima and Nagasaki. She searched the Book of
Revelation for references to Hitler. She listened to an all-
night talk show out of Los Angeles, where the conversation,

when it wasn't about communists in the State Department or fluoride in the water, was about the coming war with the Soviet Union. She told me all the Rembers would die in that war. On her globe of the earth, I watched as she traced the routes of the bombers across the North Pole.

Now, looking back forty years, it is easy to suppose that she found in me, at age five, the sort of nonskeptical audience that she lacked among her adult friends. Her other beliefs, about humans being taken up in flying saucers and about reincarnation and about the million-year-old civilizations buried beneath ocean trenches, were confided to me in tones of absolute conviction. "You're an old soul," she told me. "You know these things already."

I'm not sure if it's a good idea to tell a five-year-old he's an old soul, even if reincarnation does serve as a hedge against being vaporized. In Ketchum Elementary School I had a tough time with teachers who insisted that even though the world was about to end, I still had to do my arithmetic. Claiming soul seniority on the playground got me beatings from the schoolyard bullies, who had their own notions of hierarchy.

Even so, I was able to see what the younger souls around me either couldn't or didn't want to see. I was able to grasp how close the world was to nuclear war in 1956 and 1957 and 1958 and 1959. But with a playfulness honed by a few hundred incarnations, I decided that in this lifetime I wanted to be a nuclear physicist and make atom bombs more powerful. By the time I graduated from the eighth grade in 1964, I knew more about particle physics than anybody else in Ketchum Elementary School. I also could wrap my reincarnated mind around the fact that on any given day Russian bombers could take the polar routes and that night the falling snow would illuminate the street lamps.

During these years, I read more from my grandmother's library than from the library at school. I read books not just on nuclear physics, but on UFO cover-ups, the sunken civilizations of Mu and Atlantis, witchcraft, and soul travel to other planets. She also had a library of natural history, fine old volumes with hand-colored plates, that rationally espoused the bizarre nineteenth-century notion that all things could be known to the scientific mind. If my grandmother ever thought that there was any contradiction between her volumes on the occult, Wilhelm Reich, and the pathologies of medieval saints—I remember several volumes in a series called "Human Oddities" that focused heavily on medieval saints—and her exquisitely rational library of nineteenth-century science, she never let on about it.

Her existence during that last part of her life would have been to an old soul's reclusive liking. She grew plants, tended summer gardens, read books, and completed, in minutes, the difficult crossword puzzles in her weekly *National Observer.* She had a good mind and managed, through her books, to join a community of intellect, even if it was a community out on the ragged far edge of consensus reality.

She died when I was twelve, not of nuclear war but of cancer, after mastectomies and radiation treatments. My uncle, her son, a pathologist, burned her library. He burned her photo albums and her letters and her diaries and her diploma.

He was thorough enough in his burning that it was only thirty years later, when a cousin of my father's stopped by the ranch with a box of family photos, that I finally possessed a picture of my grandmother as a young woman. She is standing in front of a house in Hailey—I recognize the contours of Carbonate Mountain above her head—and she's a tall, handsome woman who looks straight into the camera, a half-amused smile on her face.

In the box of photos is a yellowed clipping from the Hailey newspaper: *Miss Alice W———, the well-known Twin Falls nurse, who left that city a few days ago to go to her home in Hailey on a visit, and who was reported to have mysteriously disappeared, is at Soldier, having changed her mind, and gone there for a short visit* . . .

It was the summer of 1914. She had yet to marry my grandfather and have four children, one of whom was my father. She had yet to bury a husband. She had yet to feel the full force of the tragedy that life was preparing for her. I can't be certain of the meaning of the phrase "well-known . . . nurse" but I think that at that time, if applied to a single woman who had gone missing for a number of nights but who had then turned up safe in a distant mining town, it had a tinge of disrespect for the liberties taken. In another picture I have of her, she is with my grandfather. They are young, healthy, happy, educated, respectable, beautiful, childless.

Those photos and that clipping connect—in my mind, at least—with a prematurely old and sick woman with odd books and odd plants, completing crossword puzzles in ink in a shuttered house, accompanied, during the days, by an odd impressionable child, who believed her utterly when she said that this world was too awful to bring children into.

The connection came to me in the person of my uncle, who became estranged from the rest of the family shortly after my grandmother's cremation. Fifteen years later, when I was a teacher in Sun Valley and he was there attending a pathology conference, he called me up and asked me to meet him for a drink.

Let me preface this story by saying my uncle was not a happy man. He was one of the few people I have known who had had a full-on Freudian analysis, which as it has been practiced in America is akin to skinning the soul and stretching its shimmering hide over a brutally simple and literal theoretical framework. The metaphor is not elegant, because the skinless soul does not die from this treatment but instead lives on and shows up at reunions, where it creeps out of the shadows, weeping and bloody and stinking, to wrap its forepaws around unsuspecting family members. My uncle's flayed soul was with him when I met him at Slavey's, in Ketchum, for a drink.

He told me that my grandfather had died from his profession. He had been an assayer, and the reagents that were the tools of his trade had given him liver cancer, and he died at the start of the Great Depression. The family savings, put aside for college educations, were wiped out when the banks failed. Three of the four children left home, including my father, who was fourteen when he found another family to stay with. Only my uncle, the future pathologist, was left at home. My grandmother raised him, and somehow held on to her house in Hailey and saw him through medical school.

Within this history my uncle and his analyst had arranged, in perfect order, the bloody bones of Oedipus.

I came away with a vision of what my uncle thought he was. He thought he was a golem, a puppet, a man constructed. My grandmother had begun to rage against a fate that no longer allowed her to change her destination and a world that no longer cared if she went missing for a few nights, and she had crafted a human simulacrum, an instrument to send out into that world and work her revenge upon it. She had been a nurse. My uncle was a doctor. She had been poor. He was rich. She had screamed, he told me, at her dying husband, cursing him on his deathbed. My uncle peered through a microscope at lab-prepared biopsies and diagnosed death.

"I don't have a life," he told me. "I'm living the one she wanted."

This was eighteen years after he had burned her books and had her body cremated. He had spent $50,000 on psychotherapy and as I looked across the table at him I could see her face behind his glasses. It was a tricky moment.

Since that moment I've come to an understanding of Freud that allows me to see his works as elaborate, shifting dances of veils, whole tapestries woven of hints and sly allusions. I've wished that my uncle had found a less literal-minded analyst and that Freud had found better translators.

I didn't hear from my uncle again. I remember his story, and it has allowed me to believe, in dark moments, that I carry my grandmother's soul. Perhaps that is the way reincarnation works.

But I have been luckier than my uncle, and it's been because of my own parents. I am deeply grateful that my mother found, in her career as a nurse, reason to remain convinced of her own freedom and autonomy and ability to effect change in this world without having to work through a man to do it. I'm equally grateful that my father left his mother's home when he did and only reestablished emotional contact with her after he was an adult with a family of his own.

We live in a time when tens of thousands and possibly millions of people are convinced that they have been have seized by aliens and taken to spaceships, where they have been subjected to sexual experiments. Many of these people, if they were to read the old clipping from the Hailey newspaper, would be convinced that my grandmother was also a victim of an alien abduction and very little you could say would talk them out of that conviction. Her subsequent life would be further evidence, to them, that she *had* been abducted. So it goes with such belief systems, which organize reality into elaborate, if static, crystal latticeworks.

It is doubtful that alien abductions happen in this world, but there is no doubt that they happen in the world of the psyche. Lots of people know that there are forces and beings in this world that have grabbed them, seriously messed with them, and then dumped them back into lives and selves that never again seem to belong wholly to them. If he had gone to an analyst who believed in alien abductions, my uncle would have seen my grandmother as an alien, his own life as one long abduction. He would have been happier for it.

Instead, he saw her as a witch. And when I consider what happened to her—to have gone from being a young, strong, adventurous woman with a good mind, at the dawn of a century full of promise, to being mutilated, irradiated, burned to ash at the behest of her own son, who put her books and journals into the fire—I don't think Torquemada could have done a better job of expunging her from this world. Don't let

anyone tell you that we don't still burn witches. We've simply moved the festivities from the town square to the family
hearth.

And yet my uncle, thorough as he was, failed in his efforts. My grandmother lives.

I could name all the elements in the periodic table by my first
year at Hailey High School, but it was my biology and not my
chemistry class that toured Idaho's National Reactor Testing
Station. We rode the bus through the Craters of the Moon
and Arco, through checkpoints in the desert to a cluster of
big windowless buildings. A man in white coveralls met us in
the parking lot, passed out film badges, and led us through a
tour of several reactor buildings. We walked around a great
deep pool of water that had, at its bottom, the shifting blue
glare of nuclear fire. We climbed ladders and catwalks up
to the bomb-shaped top of a reactor. We walked down long
corridors lined with pipes and dials. We listened to a lecture
about the power of the peaceful atom.

What I noticed, when I wasn't checking my badge for
signs of a lethal dose of peaceful gamma radiation, was the
absolute decay of the place. Insulation hung off pipes. The
faces of dials were dust clouded and unreadable. Dirt lay
thick on every horizontal surface. Our guide's coveralls, on
inspection, turned out to be not white but a frayed dishwater
gray, and he had the bony complexion and walk of an old
white workhorse about to be sent off to the glue works.

I never made it to senior-year physics at Hailey High. I
quit decorating my notebooks with drawings of mushroom
clouds and toppling high-rises. Some clean simplicity—made

up of definable particles and predictable interactions—that I had sought in nuclear physics was no longer there after that trip to the National Reactor Testing Station.

I should have seen it coming. I had studied half-lives and entropy. I understood that time, in this world, runs only toward messiness. I had learned of mesons, muons, and pions and if I'd only thought things through, I would have seen that the simple atomic structures I drew in study hall were about to shatter apart into ever stranger and more chaotic bits. Nuclear physics had kept me unmoving for a moment, on that awe-filled threshold where all the world is unsoiled by life, and if the bombs can be made powerful enough, it can stay that way. The dirtiness at the NRTS was the end of that illusion.

It was also the end, I think, of one of my grandmother's unlived lives. I hadn't resisted living it and had in fact lived it out to its end, following its purpose and finding that it wasn't the answer either. Not in that direction were the sweat and stink of this particular dance to be avoided.

As an aging soul, I suspect that they're not to be avoided anyway. And I think that before she died, my grandmother realized that too.

One of the things I remember from my preschool stay with her is helping her clean out a corner of her garage. It was full of old garden tools, cracked mason jars, ruptured hoses, and half-empty bottles of DDT and chlordane. Behind them all was an oval picture frame, its curved glass shattered, the pastel-tinted photo in it faded and water-stained.

I picked it up.

"Who is that?" I asked. There was a silence.

"It was me," she said.

I looked at the picture, then at her, then at the picture again. "You were *beautiful*," I said.

She looked at me and smiled. "Yes," she said, with an assurance and an ease appropriate to a woman whose changes of mind were once so important that they were reported in the newspaper. "Yes. I was beautiful."

Cache Creek, Hell's Canyon, Oregon. I'm here as a part of an ar-
chaeological SWAT team. We're determining if a Forest Service
septic system will destroy any artifacts or structures covered by the
Antiquities Act. Our methods are simple. We've dug a hundred
post holes, and have taken the dirt from them and sifted it through
eighth-inch-mesh screen. We've taken the artifacts we've found
and stored them in Zip-Loc bags. Then we've thrown the dirt back
in the holes.

Where we've found things—arrowheads, fire-cracked rock, a
harmonica reed—we've sometimes dug big holes, a meter on a side,
and taken them down ten centimeters at a time, continuing until
we run out of human sign.

We're digging in a lawn—the lawn of the Forest Service Visi-
tors' Center that sits on a high bar above the Snake River. Once it
was the lawn of a ranch house. Before that it was the site of a cor-
ral, judging from the horseshoe nails we've screened out of the dirt.

Before that it was the campsite of river-dwelling Indians. At thirty centimeters or so, we have hit a thick layer of mussel shells.

We've found five arrowheads, a trade bead, a stone pestle used to grind seeds into rough flour, lots of bent nails (we've hypothesized a tribe of cross-eyed carpenters), the fragment of harmonica, mountain-sheep bones, butcher-sawn beef T-bones, bits of bright plastic, peach pits, and shards of glass from patent-medicine bottles. Below forty-five centimeters, artifacts cease.

How many human lives are in those forty-five centimeters? Floods, climate changes, wars and migrations, and diseases are all variables that you juggle when you think about what's hidden in the shovelful of dirt on your screen. What we know for certain is that nothing we look at came from before the Bonneville Flood. Twelve thousand years ago, the ice dam holding back Lake Bonneville broke. A wall of water 1,700 feet high rushed down Hell's Canyon, washing this world down to bedrock. Everything here, even the dirt, is newer than 12,000 years.

And maybe 10,000 years ago—500 generations—humans began to camp here.

They ate mussels and T-bones and mountain sheep and peaches. They flaked delicate points for their arrows and pounded nails badly. They died of smallpox and coronaries and wounds. They sat around campfires and sang lost songs in lost tongues. They pounded grass seed into flour. They got drunk on Dr. Pierce's Favorite Prescription. They all watched the Snake slide by below them.

We've made quite a mess of the lawn and have incurred the wrath of the Visitors' Center caretaker. One of his duties is to see that the lawn stays smooth and level for visitors. The septic system that *we're scouting for them is also for those visitors, who come up from Lewiston and Asotin in roaring jet boats. They drink beer for thirty miles of river and by the time they hit Cache Creek they have to pee, and the only facility available to them is an outhouse without a roof, down by the dock. Whenever a group lands, one of them goes in and the rest stand on the hill above, pitching mostly empty beer cans into the open top of the outhouse and making rude noises. The Forest Service doesn't approve of such goings-on at its Visitors' Centers. Hence the proposed septic system, with proposed flush toilets, in proposed separate rooms—one for men and one for women.*

There is a flush toilet here already, in the caretaker's cabin, but he won't let visitors use it. He won't let us use it either. He's forbidden us the use of the shower too, and we've been digging here in the heat and the dirt for five days. We've taken to bathing in the Snake, but it's a cold and worrisome hygiene.

We don't mention the Flood to the caretaker because he's a fundamentalist Christian. If we were to point out the high marks on the canyon walls that Lake Bonneville made when it passed by here, he would come to a very different interpretation of the data, one all about Noah and the cleansing of a corrupt world. He doesn't believe that anything here in Hell's Canyon is older than 4,000 years. Two hundred generations. Fewer, if you consider that some of the folks in Genesis weren't even into puberty until they were ninety.

And there's nothing in our plastic bags that casts any doubt on Genesis. The stone points we've found are all Late Prehistoric, from a thousand or two years ago. We have no evidence of those earlier, higher cultures, rumored to have been led by artisan-hunters, whose lives were given meaning when they killed a mammoth and

33

whose art survives as delicate, astonishingly beautiful Folsom points. We have no carbon dates, no mammoth ivory, no fragments of woven reeds—nothing from before any flood.

Will the septic system destroy valuable evidence of a vanished people? There will never be a definite answer. We have to guess, and because we haven't hit anything like rune-inscribed stones or Lewis and Clark goodwill medallions or the golden plates of the Mormons, our report will give its blessing: Put Your Septic System Here.

But still, there are the shell middens and the long warm days that never shook with the roar of jet boats, the distant sound of a harmonica, the mountain sheep that fell to arrows, and the once-new corral, its nails driven with the force of a bent dream. There are the necklaces of beads and the rocks that ringed fire. Each bite of the shovel touches a life, and each handful of earth breathes back at you.

Hunting Lessons

ONE MORNING a few years ago I was hunting the breaks around Huckleberry Creek in the foothills of the Sawtooths, across from Obsidian. When I had left my father at a fork in the trail, the last thing he had said was, "Whatever you do, don't shoot an ugly stinking old bull." I nodded agreement, because ugly stinking old bulls take up lots of space in the freezer and you end up eating gamy hamburger for a year.

At the edge of a meadow, an hour later, I crept up on the ugliest old bull elk I had ever seen, in a zoo or out of one. I lay down on the other side of a log and watched him instead of killing him. He was about twenty-five feet away, and I counted seven points on each of his antlers. He was snorting and sniffing and nervous. Both his rear legs were urine stained and he was looking away from me, into thick trees. I finally saw what he was looking at a hundred feet away, a small spike bull. I squirmed this way and that, trying to get the spike in my scope, but all I could see were lodgepoles in the crosshairs. Ten minutes passed.

Then there was a gunshot, and the big bull fell over. He flopped around for a few seconds, then struggled to his feet and ran off into the trees. I jumped up, trying to see the spike, and ran after him.

Someone began screaming. "Stay away from my elk! Stay away from my elk, you son of a bitch!" I stopped and watched while a hunter, rifle ready, in camo-print pants and a gray sweater ran up to me.

"That's my elk," he said. "I killed it."

I nodded in agreement.

"I didn't want your elk," I said. "I wanted the spike bull behind him." The spike was long gone.

"What spike bull?" he asked.

"Behind him. I've been watching the one you shot for ten minutes."

His eyes went hard and dead. "No you haven't," he said.

"Have too," I said.

"No. You haven't. You would have shot him."

"I didn't want an ugly stinking old bull," I said.

He stared at me. "Don't touch my elk," he said.

I didn't want to touch anything of his. I knew that if I did, he would shoot me. I also thought he might shoot me if I convinced him I didn't want to touch his elk. He walked away into the lodgepoles, to where his elk had fallen down again, and I went looking for my father to see if his luck had been any better than mine.

.   .   .

My father had not always been so selective. When I was seven years old, he took me across the river at dusk in early September. He had his rifle, an elk whistle, and a small backpack that contained knives, a hatchet, and a rope hoist. We rode across the river on bundles of canvas tied onto a packsaddle carried by our old mare, Doll. We were out of meat. It was a month before the start of elk season. What we were doing, my father told me, was poaching.

We went a mile toward the Sawtooths, following a game trail through the trees until we came to a large meadow, red and orange and tan against the black-green of lodgepole. My father whistled for an elk and one answered quickly. Another whistle, another answer. Within a few minutes, a large dark shape moved away from the wall of forest and began trotting toward us in the slanted light.

It was an old and angry bull. He stopped fifty yards from where we were hidden at the meadow's edge and whistled once more. He had his head down and his neck outstretched, and he was shaking his antlers when my father broke his neck with a bullet.

The report from the shot echoed for a long moment before fading to silence. My father scanned the edges of the meadow for any movement. But we were alone, which was a good thing.

My father cut the elk's throat and then tied a pack rope from Doll's saddle to its hind legs. I grasped Doll's halter rope and led her far enough to drag the elk into the trees. There my father gutted it, hoisted it off the ground, cut its head off, and skinned it.

He used the hatchet to split it in two vertically, working on the spinal column from inside the body cavity, splitting each vertebra with a hatchet stroke or two, then moving on to the next. It was my job to stand behind him and spread the front legs when he had worked his way down to the shoulders, in order to keep already shattered bone out of the way of bone about to be shattered. When he was done, I was almost as bloody as he was.

We cut the two halves of the carcass into quarters, wrapped the hindquarters in canvas, and packed them on Doll. It was dark, but the eastern horizon was beginning to glow from a rising moon. In that light, horses can see better than men. My father tied Doll's halter rope to her saddle and told her to go home, and we followed her back down the game trail to the river. We waded it behind her, and she picked her way through the river-bottom willows to our backyard fence. We unloaded her and hung the meat in the back room of the house. It was my bedtime. I went to bed, and my father rode Doll back across the river for the front quarters of the elk.

Over the next few weeks, after I went to bed, my mother and father spent hours in our kitchen cutting up the elk and packaging it. When they were done, our freezer was full.

"It's tough old elk," my father said at dinner that winter. "But not as tough as no tough old elk at all."

Most of what I remember from this incident is how to gut a male ungulate. After you cut through the thick hair around the throat and sever the jugular and carotid vessels so the blood will drain and not spoil the meat, you grasp the penis and skin it away from the body back to where it enters the pelvic bones near the anus. The penis is much longer than you might expect, and as soon as you get it free from the skin, you tie a knot in it so no urine will leak from it and spoil any meat.

Then, in an even more delicate operation, you cut around the anus with a gentle stabbing motion to free it from the large gluteal muscles. Then you open up the body cavity by slicing open the thin skin of the lower abdomen all the way to the sternum. You reach in and grab the anus and penis from the inside, pinching the anus shut so no feces will spoil the meat.

You pull them out through the slit in the abdomen, and the intestines and liver and kidneys come with them. Then you slice away the diaphragm to get to the lungs and heart, which have their own attachments to the rest of the carcass. These must be carefully cut, and then the lungs and heart have to be pulled out along with the windpipe, which should have been severed when the throat was cut. It's important to remove the windpipe because it's full of bacteria, which, if left to breed in the body cavity, will spoil the meat.

I did not know this language when I was a seven-year-old poacher. It came much later and attached itself to blood and tendons and the spreading blue wounds that followed the glint of steel. It attached itself to journeys across the river when the freezer was empty, to the quick inspections of darkening meadows and clearings after single, too loud shots to the heads or necks of deer and elk, and to our family's alert attention to the Idaho Fish and Game pickups when they went by on the highway.

On a fall morning just after my tenth birthday, I rode Doll up the ridge on the north side of Gold Creek behind my father. He was riding Nancy, our brood mare. In the rifle scabbard under my leg was a .30-30 Winchester carbine. I had learned how to use it in the backyard, shooting at hand-drawn targets thumbtacked to firewood rounds. I had a sack of deformed bullets in my bedroom that I had painstakingly collected by splitting the firewood into smaller and smaller pieces until the bullets fell free. It was deer season, but I was too young for a license and tag.

We stopped at a small rock-piled knoll halfway up the ridge and spotted a herd of fifteen deer walking single file across a sagebrush-covered slope. They were across several small gullies from us. We got back on the horses, and I was warned for the fourth or fifth time not to shoot off the back of Doll. It wasn't that she would spook and run. It was that shooting that close to her head would be hard on her ears.

When we had ridden half the distance to the deer, we got off the horses. My father motioned me to go ahead of him. He told me the deer were 200 yards away and that I should aim the gun a foot above their backs at that range. I sat down with the carbine, picked out a deer, aimed at it, and pulled the trigger. The gun kicked against my shoulder and a puff of dust rose from a sagebrush a yard downhill from the deer I had aimed at.

They all began moving a little faster. I shot again, this time above them. Two more shots missed. The lead deer stopped, looking uphill. I missed again. A doe tumbled downhill with the next shot, but she got back up on three legs and limped back into the herd, trailing a leg broken at the knee. She was now my deer. I would have to follow her all day and night, if necessary, to kill her and bring her home.

I had to reload. When I had six more shells in the carbine I shot again at the doe. But the deer next to her, a spike buck, fell down. I shot five more times, raising dust. The deer milled this way and that, unsure of where the bullets were coming from. It wasn't until my fourteenth shot that I hit my deer in the ribcage.

"That's enough," said my father.

When we reached the deer, I slit their throats with the hunting knife I had received as a birthday present. Then I gutted them while my father watched. I was slow and a couple of times I nicked intestines but got them out of the body cavity before they spoiled any meat. I cut the antlers off the buck and my father put them in his backpack. When I was finally done, we placed the deer in canvas sacks, slung them over the saddles of the horses, and tied them down. Doll was used to this sort of thing, but Nancy snorted and kicked, and we had to load her twice.

Then we led the horses back down to the ranch. It was getting dark. At the highway, we found a spot where the trees came close to the blacktop on both sides, waited until we didn't hear any vehicles, and then crossed. The steel of the horseshoes clapped loud against the pavement. We worked our way up through the willows to the backyard and hung the deer in the back room.

My mother hadn't heard us come into the yard, but she heard us in the back room and asked from the kitchen if we'd had any luck.

"John got two deer," my father said. "We're lucky he didn't get fourteen."

I was twelve. I had a hunting license and a deer tag, and I was riding beside my father. We were far up Ohio Gulch, which runs east from the Wood River Valley between Ketchum and

Hailey. We had driven past the Blaine County landfill, climbing through the bitter smoke of fires banked by plastic and garbage to the place where the road became rough and rocky. A few miles later, the hillsides steepened to forty-five degrees, narrowing the sky, and a mile after that came great rock outcrops and hoodoos that narrowed the sky even further. It was beside one of these outcrops that my father spotted a small four-point buck.

It was a 1,000-foot climb. This time I had my mother's gun, which, with its high-powered scope, was accurate at that distance. But it was worth the effort to get closer and try for a head shot.

I began by climbing up a small draw on the other side of the outcrop. I took my time, moving quietly and smoothly up the hillside, climbing out of the sight and hearing of the buck. When I was sure I was above him, I climbed out on a rock ledge and spotted him fifty yards below. He was standing still, looking down at our Jeep.

I sat down on the rock and got into a comfortable kneeling position. The deer still didn't move. I released the safety and found his head in the scope.

He wasn't quite a statue. I could see him breathe. But he didn't act the way deer were supposed to act during hunting season. Most of the deer I had killed up to that time had been like the first two. They had sensed danger and were moving nervously around when I shot them. Because they were moving, I had aimed for the rib cage, just back of the shoulder. It was a shot that spoiled meat, but it almost always brought them down. A clean head shot, however, was just that—clean.

I stood up and moved forward on the rock, to a point where I knew my father could see me shooting. I could see the barrel of his rifle sticking out of the window of the Jeep toward me, and I knew he was watching me and the deer through his own scope. I knew I was on a pedestal of broken rock and I had a momentary vision of myself, taller and stronger than I had been before, standing against a deep sky. It was the first time I had imagined myself as I might look through my father's eyes, and it was a surprise that he might be seeing me on any kind of pedestal. I knelt again, found the buck's ear in my crosshairs, and fired at a spot an inch below it.

The buck's hind legs gave an enormous last bound, pushing the rest of him up and out, ten feet over open space. He hit yards downhill, dead, rolling end over end half a dozen times. I climbed down to where he stopped, and because the hillside was so steep, I was able to grasp one side of his antlers and pull him downhill at a run. When I got to the bottom of the gulch, my father met me. He was happy and a little relieved. He told me it was a good approach and a good shot, but he wanted to know why I had gone so far out on the rock. From where he had been, he said, it looked as though I was about to fall off.

Then he said, "Something's wrong with your deer."

It was true. The steepness of the hill wasn't the only reason I had been able to drag the buck down so easily. There was very little to him except hair and bones and antlers. It was a time of year when deer are supposed to be fat, but he was a Giacometti deer, reduced to the last thing that can be called a deer before it becomes something else. When I opened up his abdomen, the tumor was there, gray-black and ropy, wound around the stomach, embedded in the diaphragm, knotted up against the backbone.

"What do I do?" I asked.

Something worse than disgust crossed my father's face. "Leave him. He's been dying a long time."

I wanted to cut the antlers off, but my father wouldn't let me. "We'll find another buck for you," he said. "Let's get out of here."

The deer I killed that fall was a doe. In the garage, however, hanging with the hundreds of antlers my father had brought home, were the tiny antlers from the first buck I had ever killed. I took comfort in them.

Four years later I quit hunting for a long time. During those four years I seldom hit the deer I shot at, because I always tried for head shots. I shot for heads at 1,000 yards and at heads barely visible through thick alder and brush. I shot for heads when animals were running hard away from me. I shot at heads when I couldn't see heads at all. I remember that once my father decided that I was missing on purpose and that it must be because I didn't like the blood and stench of gutting. He told me that if I could just kill something he'd take care of it.

But that didn't help. I kept on aiming at heads and missing. When I was sixteen I told him that I didn't want to hunt anymore. He nodded, accepting what I said easily enough that there was no mistaking that he thought I was a far different person than he was, living in a far different world, and that he was a little relieved that I was. When I finally did go hunting with him again, he was an old man, and he was a different person then, living in a different world.

The cancer-ridden deer haunted me for several years. What haunts me now is my father's reaction to it. I had never seen him revolted by anything before, and it's taken me a long time to hypothesize why he didn't even want that deer's antlers in his garage. I think now that it brought a terrifying short halt to his careful moves around danger and death. They were moves he was trying to teach me but I was a slow learner, too much in need of words to understand things. The language he dealt in was full of glides and sudden drops and sharp upward turns toward the sky, and it didn't have words at all.

Now I live in a world where people show elk and deer antlers to other people, saying, in a language of bone, "here is a mysterious, magical animal that I've hunted, killed, and brought home." Unfortunately, languages can lie, and the language of bone is no exception. Out in the hills this year, I've found three complete bull elk skeletons with their antlers chopped off. The rest of their bones were undisturbed, which means that they were likely killed for their antlers and the meat was left to rot.

Even so, when I go out to my parents' garage and stand under the antler points that hang down from the ceiling joists like stalactites, my father stands under them with me. He grins at me and points at the tiny rack of a spike buck.

During his last few hunting seasons, my father invited the hunters who stopped by his house out to the garage to see the antlers, promising to show them a six-by-seven rack. In the language of big-game trophies, that's a rack with six points on one side and seven on the other, and it always comes with a story because deer and elk don't grow that kind of rack without surviving many hunting seasons avoiding hunters with less wit and strength and stamina.

But then he would take the little rack down and tell the visitors that it was a six- by seven-*inch* rack. Then he'd start telling stories about the other antlers hanging there, and it would be hours before they all came back to the house.

That little six-by-seven rack came from a buck he killed on a river-bottom ranch down near Challis. The rancher let him drive his pickup through the fields and pastures to the cottonwood-covered islands in the floodplain. My mother was with him, and they drove over a side channel and found the herd that stayed there year round, protected by fences and No Trespassing signs. My father stepped out of the pickup and killed the buck. They gutted it, loaded it in the back of the pickup, drove it home, hung it for a week, and then cut it up. They both were in their late seventies.

Out in the garage, some of the antlers have tags that go back to 1943. Some of them are huge. Some of them come with stories of nights spent out in snowstorms, of long walks out when cars or pickups broke down or got high-centered on stumps, of long-dead friends, of easy shots missed and impossible shots made.

"Come on out to the garage," my father would tell the visiting hunters. "I'll show you a true six-by-seven." He spoke in an odd and rare dialect of the language of bone, one suitable for jokes, sly hints, sudden reversals, and the blunting of the sharp truths of old age.

I don't know to what degree our family's survival in Sawtooth Valley depended on keeping our freezer full of elk and deer meat regardless of the season. I can remember evenings when my mother and father huddled at the kitchen table over stacks of bills and receipts, calculating a way to pay the $75 they owed each month on the ranch. It may have been that a few dollars one way or another would have made the difference between the whole family staying where we were or moving back to Hailey for mortgage payments and year-round, full-time employment in the service of someone else's enterprise.

When my father had left the Triumph Mine in 1953, his friends underground had told him that he would be back. "You won't make it on your own out there," they said.

Of course, they were right. Without my mother's management of the finances, he—and we—wouldn't have made it. She maximized every dollar he brought in as a fishing guide. She had a horror of debt. The ranch was, as far as I know, the last thing they bought on credit, and that was fifty years ago. She had been brought up on a farm in the Great Depression and still remembers with a smoldering anger being teased by the town children because she had only one skirt and one blouse to wear to school, and she wore them every day. Even now, when she has enough money to live well for the rest of her life, she worries over the phone and power and gas bills, as if the $200 they take from her account each month will break her. It doesn't help that she knows other eighty-five-year-olds for whom that gray terror is real. Some of them are the same people who teased her when she was a third-grader.

But I suspect that my father, by taking one more fishing client or setting one more line of traps, could have made up the difference in cost between a poached elk and a side of beef. Certainly, if he had ever gotten caught, he would have lost his guide's license, his trapping license, and his ability to make a living in the valley, and that would have settled the matter then and there.

Tom Spintree was the name of the game warden assigned to Sawtooth Valley. I met him one day, as an eight-year-old, when we were ice fishing at Jimmy Smith Lake on the East Fork of the Salmon. It was a cold day in January. We had driven over Galena Summit, checked the buildings at the ranch, and then had gone another sixty miles to the lake. We got there at two in the afternoon, just in time to watch the sun go down behind the southwest horizon. The temperature dropped below zero.

Jimmy Smith is a shallow lake, in most places less than ten feet deep, but in January its ice lies three feet thick. That day, as usual, there were plenty of holes in it, augered there by people who had become tired of watching a willow pole shake to the rhythm of their shivering and had decided to do something productive with their time. I broke the inch of ice that covered the surface of one hole, found a discarded ice-fishing rig—a willow, eight feet of heavy monofilament salmon line, a sinker, and a hook—and baited it with corn. Almost immediately I felt a tug, and when I lifted the pole upward, I had a fish on.

For Jimmy Smith Lake, it was huge. Most of the fish there were six or eight inches, brook trout, but this one, when I jerked him to the surface, was a full sixteen inches, a fish that had finally grown big enough to eat the other brook trout, which had assured it of a steady supply of protein. It was humped, with a curved snout and teeth like a Doberman's. I yelled and looked around to the other holes to where my brother, father, and mother had been huddling over their own fishing holes, and saw that a big man was talking with my father. My father took out his wallet and showed the man his license, and they both walked over to me to check out my fish, which I had killed by hitting its head on the ice three or four times.

"You got a license for that fish?" said the man. Only then did I realize that it was Spintree, the game warden. I knew his name, even though I had never met him. He figured large in my father's salmon fishing stories. Spintree would put on overalls and irrigating boots, throw a shovel over his shoulder, and walk the banks of the Salmon River. He'd arrest the southern Idaho farmers who came up from the flatlands and snagged or speared salmon. His costume was a perfect predator's camouflage. The farmers saw Spintree as one of their own hired hands, even though there wasn't an irrigation ditch within miles.

Spintree hunted men as other men hunted elk and deer. My father was one of the men he hunted, and suddenly I knew he was hunting me too.

I didn't have a license. I didn't need one. A fishing license became necessary when you were twelve. Up to that time, the fish you caught, unlike the deer you killed, were added to the limits of the people who were with you who did have licenses.

But looking up at Spintree, I forgot all that. I remembered instead poaching with my father and all the other poaching stories, some of them from times before I was born, and I was sure I was about to go to jail.

I reached down, grabbed the big fish off the ice, and threw it back in the hole. It broke through the thin film of ice that had formed since I'd caught it, drifted down into the narrowing darkness, and was gone.

"What did you do that for?" asked my father.

Spintree laughed. "He got rid of the evidence," he said. He grinned at my father. "Is this your kid?" Then he looked at me and said, "Don't ever waste a fish like that again. If you do, I'll have to arrest your dad."

My father was angry. He reached into his fishing bag and extracted one of the big treble hooks that he used for salmon fishing in the summer. He gave it to me.

"Put this on your line," he said. "See if you can snag your fish."

I spent the rest of that short bleak day dipping that bare hook into the water, dragging it around until it snagged something, then pulling it back up. I caught willow branches gnawed clean of bark by beaver and muskrat, a couple of plastic bait jugs, and several hundred feet of monofilament line. But the fish was gone. Spintree had left us after talking with my father about trapping season. He'd checked the licenses of the other people on the lake and then had walked back to the warmth of his pickup and had driven back to Stanley.

I had broken a law. It's against the law to waste game in Idaho. But Spintree hadn't done anything.

I had also violated a family rule, which was that you never wasted game even if the law said you could. You never took a fish or a deer or an elk if you weren't going to eat it.

During the long dark ride back to Hailey, the car was silent. Six or seven small fish were riding in the trunk. My father did not speak to me. I thought about the evil that had suddenly sprouted within me and tried to figure out why it felt so awful. Looking back to that time, I realize that my throwing the fish back into Jimmy Smith Lake had upset a delicate relationship between my father and Spintree. Our family had entered into Spintree's debt, and it wasn't a debt that would be easily forgiven.

Throwing away my prize fish had called forth a thing from within Spintree that neither he nor we had a name for, but it was a thing cunning and cruel. The next summer he drove up to our house when my father was out hunting. It was late August. Deer hunting season was six weeks away. He knocked on our door and asked my mother where my father was, and when she said he was away on a welding job, he said he'd wait for him if she didn't mind. She made him tea, and he sat and drank it while my mother kept up a bright conversation about the salmon fishing clients we'd had that summer, and we all waited there for my father to come home and be arrested.

He didn't come home, of course. Coming down from the mountains above the place, he had spotted the green pickup in our driveway and had taken his deer downriver, to a neighbor's place, and he called home to tell my mother that he'd be late and not to wait dinner on him. My mother told Spintree that my father would be late and, as she had to start cooking, he couldn't wait there any longer.

Spintree got up, moving slowly as he always did, and smiled to show he understood what it meant that he wasn't invited for dinner. As he was leaving, he looked on a shelf beside the kitchen stove and saw the curing pelt of a chuckar partridge that my brother had left there to dry. He picked it up, ruffled its feathers, didn't say anything, and put it back down. When he had left, I remember my mother saying,

"That damned bird!" She had presumed it was an illegal kill, but chuckar season had opened, and my brother had shot and skinned it only a few days before on the East Fork, not far from Jimmy Smith Lake. After Spintree's visit my mother kept the bits and pieces of dead animals that lay around our house to a minimum.

The summer after that, Spintree tried to arrest a big flat-lander on the river. The man had illegally snagged a salmon. Spintree had sat on the bank above and behind the man, and when the salmon was on solid ground had flashed his badge and reached down for the fish, saying, "That's not your fish. That's my fish."

The man dropped his pole, grabbed Spintree by his belt and collar, and pitched him out into deep swift water. Spin-tree couldn't swim. It was a while before he was pulled out of the water and a while before they got him breathing again. The evidence escaped to spawn and die, and Spintree never made his arrest.

My father repeated this story year after year, long after Spintree had been transferred, and long after he had died. Spintree never pressed charges against the man who threw him in the river. It turned out that when the man wasn't competing in amateur weight-lifting competitions, he was a police officer, which may have been the reason that the matter ended where it did.

But it's more likely that Spintree was just embarrassed. He took a rough pride in his work and he had made an error in judgment. I'm sure he would have liked the story to have been forgotten. It would have been, except that my father kept bringing it up again and again, usually telling it to the crowd at the public hearings put on by the Idaho Department of Fish and Game.

When I think about Spintree now, I see him as one of those big awkward slow-moving kids in school who get teased a lot until they get big enough to hurt someone, and then they become unwilling, low-grade bullies. As adults, they cause little kids to cry with their teasing. Many of them drift into law enforcement as though it's the dark slot at the bottom of the pinball machine they're stuck in, and they spend the rest of their lives halfway between being cruel to people and wanting their respect and friendship.

I think my father understood Spintree and his particular vulnerability, had liked and respected him, and had played a kind of game with him until I threw that fish into the water. It wasn't Spintree's fault that the game ended. It wasn't mine either, or my father's. It was just an incident that forced their attention onto the fundamental unforgiving antagonism that lay between them.

That was forty-five years ago. In the winter of 1981, long after my father quit poaching, the Idaho poacher Claude Dallas killed two game wardens who were arresting him for the illegal taking of bobcats. He had shot both men in the head after wounding them, and after that, game wardens in Idaho packed handguns on their belts and high-powered rifles and shotguns in their pickups.

My father must have known how quickly things could have turned deadly when he was poaching, and how badly it could have turned out for him and the rest of us. But he did it anyway, placing himself outside the law in an act so deliberate it became ceremony. As he grew older, though, he poached less and less and finally stopped. He hunted legally, trapped legally, and fished legally. When he got old enough, the State of Idaho gave him his fishing and hunting licenses for nothing, in a small geriatric way restoring his outlaw status. It made him happy, but it was a happiness that held the bright, confected odor of nostalgia. Toward the end of his life he was unable to hunt at all, and the local game warden gave him seized elk and deer meat. It had been taken from hunters caught in the act of killing a doe in a buck-only hunt or a cow elk in a bull-only hunt.

"I've got a freezer full of poached meat again," my father would say. He would grin. "We'll make it through the winter."

"You'd probably make it through the winter without it," I'd say.

"It wouldn't be good to have to find out," he'd say.

First Date

M Y MOTHER'S GUN is a .257 Roberts. It's a sporting rifle with a scope and a Mauser action, capable of accelerating a 100-grain .25 caliber bullet to 3,000 feet per second. It's accurate to 1,000 yards, although in the mountains around our home, a 1,000-yard shot means work. It is often the start of a long day of climbing up or down to an elk or deer, gutting and hanging the carcass, walking back to the pasture for a horse, riding a packsaddle back up to the meat, and packing it out, sometimes in daylight, sometimes not.

I've passed up shots I could have made and made shots I should have passed up. Once when a bull elk was running a half-mile across a deep canyon from me, I put the crosshairs of the .257 between his antlers and squeezed the trigger. He fell down and I found the bullet lying free on his tongue. That elk came out in the daylight, but it was daylight of the next day.

I have the gun now because my mother quit hunting one

day when she and my father were out road hunting and drove by a small buck standing in a roadside meadow. My mother said that when she looked into the buck's eyes through the scope she found herself unable to pull the trigger. She handed the gun back to my father—it had been his gift to her at the start of their marriage—who in an act of complete wisdom said the buck was hers if it was anybody's and that he wouldn't kill it for her. They came home without a deer.

Later that fall, when I was twelve and old enough to legally hunt with my father, the .257 was the gun I carried. However misguided it might seem now, I looked at carrying my mother's gun as proof that I had completed a rite of passage into manhood. I thought of myself as a man—a twelve-year-old man but a man nonetheless—who was good with a rifle. It took me a while to see that the gun wasn't the key to manhood that I thought it was. That understanding occurred at the age of fourteen, when I brought it along on my first date.

In the early sixties the valley was a place where land with river frontage and a view of the Sawtooth Mountains could still be purchased for a few hundred dollars an acre. It had yet to become the Sawtooth National Recreation Area, and trophy houses had yet to spring up in its meadows and on its hilltops. The jobs available in Stanley paid little. The people who held them were quite often people down on their luck, who drove into town in big old cars with cracked windshields and ruptured mufflers, who took dishwashing, irrigating, and sawmill jobs for six weeks or a month—sometimes only for as long as it took to get a headgasket or a water pump replaced—and then left for the higher pay that could be had in Boise or Portland or Salt Lake. There were two distinct communities in the valley then, the people who had property there, who were permanent, and the people who worked for them, who weren't. Now the workers stay through the winters and the people whose houses they caretake drive their sport utilities up and down Highway 75 for a few weeks every summer.

But the summer I was fourteen the old woman who managed the café at the Stanley Club—the old Stanley Club, with the wagon-wheel railings out front, before it burned down—brought along her niece Corinna, who was just my age, to waitress for her. Corinna, according to the town gossips, was with her aunt because of a bad home life.

Corinna had dark hair, smooth skin, bright blue eyes, and a quick unhappy smile that showed white, even teeth. She was, to my fourteen-year-old eyes, amazingly grown up. She looked ten years older than I did, and it wasn't just her makeup that made her look that way. A deep anger and toughness lay beneath the adult curves of her body. I could tell you now about the bad home she came from, but then I didn't have a clue. I just thought she was beautiful and mysterious. I also thought that if she were ever to start thinking of me the way I was thinking of her, we would probably get married and go to high school together.

I began to spend time in the Stanley Club when Corinna was working. I had gotten my driver's license that summer. Every other day I would drive my father's Jeep—which I had the use of until he needed it for trapping in the fall—down the valley to town, where I would spend my fence-building money on hamburgers and Cokes. Other men ate at the

Stanley Club because of Corinna, but they were all twenty or twenty-five years old, and Corinna's aunt would run them off the minute they asked her out.

I was tolerated, perhaps because I was fourteen, perhaps because the look of stupid fascination on my face had entertainment value, or perhaps because my future looked less harmful than that of the men who sat on either side of me at the counter. When I finally got up nerve enough to ask Corinna for a date, somewhere in the middle of July, she said yes.

"Where will we go?" she asked. There wasn't a lot to do in Stanley if you were fourteen, especially in the daylight, and I couldn't drive after dark. Corinna had been able to get into the bars until her aunt told all the bartenders how old she was.

"We'll go hunting," I said.

Corinna looked at me skeptically. But whatever I had to offer was better than sitting in her aunt's cabin after her morning shift, watching snowy Boise soap operas on a nine-inch black-and-white TV set.

"Bring some beer," she said.

My parents gave up early on the idea that I would turn out like them at all. They knew that religious fundamentalist parents end up raising homosexuals, pacifist parents end up with pictures of marines on their mantels, the children of doctors end up as ski bums, ranchers raise environmental activists, environmental activists raise religious fundamentalists. It's a near-universal process, and only the ignorant or the foolish blame parents for deliberately crafting the people their children become.

Which is to say that my parents shouldn't be blamed for deliberately creating me, or, more specifically, me as a fourteen-year-old in a four-wheel-drive vehicle, with a high-powered rifle in the gun rack, fifty rounds of ammunition and two six-packs of beer on the floorboards, and a fourteen-year-old girl in the passenger seat.

At that time there was a store in the valley where you could buy beer if you had the money and were tall enough to put it on the counter. The day of our date, Corinna's aunt was working a double shift. I stopped at the store on my way into town and bought two six-packs of Coors. I had told my parents I was going rockchuck hunting, leaving out the parts about Corinna and the beer. Rockchuck hunting was an accepted family prelude to elk season, even if it did mean killing animals that were not going to be eaten.

After picking up Corinna at her aunt's cabin, I drove the Jeep out of Stanley and across the Valley Creek Bridge to the rocky slope under the bluff that sits a quarter-mile north of town. It's an area of houses now, houses that sit on flat gouges in the hillside, but then the only mark of human habitation was the Stanley cemetery. I parked the Jeep where we had a clear view of the rocks. Corinna had opened a beer the moment she got into the Jeep, and she got out with it, climbed onto the hood and leaned back against the windshield.

At that stage in my drinking career I didn't think I liked beer—since then, I've realized I just don't like Coors—and I had an idea that it might affect my marksmanship. I waved away the beer she opened for me and sat in front of her on the bumper of the Jeep, waiting for movement in the rocks above.

"I've never been on a date like this before," said Corinna, about the time I found a rockchuck in my crosshairs.

I couldn't think of an intelligent reply. "There's one," I said, and pulled the trigger.

The gunshot echoed off the rocks and only a little later, off the buildings of Stanley. Corinna gave a little yelp. Where the rockchuck had been was a drifting cloud of green mist, the remains of the grass it had been eating that morning.

"That's disgusting," Corinna said. "Why don't you just come up here and have a beer?"

But I couldn't. A horrible self-consciousness had come over me. I found myself looking over my own shoulder, and I didn't like what I saw. The success of the whole afternoon had depended on her approving of my killing rockchucks and maybe on her killing a couple herself. But she didn't approve. She didn't see the hidden connections between a rockchuck slaughter and nurturing family, meat on the table, a safe place in the world. I suddenly knew that the easy conversations we had had in the Stanley Club café—mostly one-sided, about my starting high school and what sort of job I would have after college—were over. She was drinking a second beer and looking at me through critical eyes and seeing, I thought, a little boy with a gun.

Unfortunately, I was also a little boy with no idea of how to act on his first date except for some preconceptions that were proving horribly wrong. I had an idea that I might present her with the dead rockchuck as a sort of trophy, so I ran up into the rocks after it. But when I got to where it had been, I couldn't find any identifiable pieces.

By the time I got back to the gun, a second rockchuck appeared atop a rock and since I didn't know what else to do, I shot it.

"Stop that!" said Corinna. "He didn't do anything to you."

"He's a rockchuck," I said.

"Come here," she said. I reluctantly put the gun in the cab of the Jeep and climbed up on the hood beside her. She handed me another open beer.

"I'm three ahead of you," she said. "You'd better catch up."

I wordlessly choked down a beer, and when I saw that she was still three ahead of me, another.

Then Corinna said, "Well, you've got me where you want me." She kissed me and took off her shirt. Corinna had come with preconceptions too, even if it wasn't her first date.

"You should put that back on," I said, and not just because I realized at that moment that the hidden connections Corinna was following led to a place in the world that was not safe. I was also looking up over the top of the Jeep to where the deputy sheriff for the south end of Custer County was slowly driving his cruiser down the dirt road toward us. Beside him, in the passenger seat, was Corinna's aunt.

Corinna got her shirt back on just in time for her aunt and the deputy to grab her and put her in the back of the cruiser.

"You stay right here, son," said the deputy. "Don't you move an inch." He drove Corinna and her aunt back across Valley Creek and into town. He was back in two minutes. He looked into the cab of the Jeep and, reaching in, grabbed the other six-pack.

"Where'd you get the beer?" he asked.

I told him.

He nodded. "You get the hell home," he said. "Right now." He looked in the Jeep again. "Nice gun," he said.

"It's my mom's," I said.

My father never mentioned my first date, except to suggest that there might be places to hunt rockchucks a little farther from the center of Stanley. I quit going into town for lunch. I didn't buy any more beer that summer. The deputy stopped me on the highway one day, checked my learner's permit, looked behind the seats in the Jeep, handled the gun in the gun rack, and asked me if I wanted to sell it. I told him no and he let me go.

Corinna was not so lucky. She was, I heard, suddenly allowed to date twenty-five-year-olds. She finally settled on one of them, a grinning little guy named Eddie who washed dishes at the Rod and Gun Club and drove an old Cadillac that blew smoke and had plywood for rear side windows. She left town with him in August and that was the last time I saw her. I heard later that she was having a baby and that she and Eddie had gotten married. A girlfriend said she was living in a trailerhouse in Wyoming while Eddie looked for work in the uranium mines around Flaming Gorge.

That fall I killed a deer on my fifteenth birthday, but there was little manhood in the act. I had learned that the magic can fall out of things and that you can be involved in rites of passage that turn out to be all about somebody else. I had learned that Corinna's toughness wasn't much armor against the dangers she faced. And I had figured out that the reason I hadn't gotten into trouble for buying beer was either that the store owner would have gotten into much bigger trouble for selling it to me or that the deputy liked Coors.

For a while I had been young enough to be able to see myself as an adult. But by the end of my fifteenth year I realized that my status was more ambiguous. Hidden connections, more than I ever suspected, lay between the structures of my world. My father's life as a trapper and as a fishing and hunting guide, for instance, required doctors, lawyers, and financiers and the complex imaginary universe of science and law that gave their lives meaning. For a few days, his job was to maintain their illusion that a simple life grounded in the real was possible. His clients gave him real cash to maintain that illusion. Almost all of who I was had been formed by a studied unreality.

And that is why I brought a gun along on my first date.

Late one afternoon that November, when I was accompanying my father on his trapline out Valley Creek, we came upon a tree he used as a landmark for mink and marten sets. The tree was memorable because set into its trunk was a black-and-white photograph covered by Plexiglas. Bark had healed around the picture and framed it with smooth living tissue. It was a wonder, a window, a passage into memory.

The picture was of a man in uniform, a woman in a cotton print dress, and a naked child.

That fall, for the first time, I realized that the bark would eventually cover the picture. Half of the man was covered already, and I understood that there would be a moment in the future when I might look closely at a dimple in the bark of the tree and see, at the bottom of it, an eye.

Then I remembered that the people in the photograph were no longer young. The child was older than me by a decade. World War II could have ripped the man and woman apart forever. Either one of them could be dead of a bad heart or alcohol or cancer or grief or craziness. Or they could be alive and old enough to have forgotten that they had ever framed a photograph with a tree.

It was not hard, in that moment, to see Corinna and Eddie and his Cadillac framed by bark, caught smiling in the bright flash of good luck turning bad. It was not hard to see my father, unbelievably young, preserved by Plexiglas, presenting my mother—a girl—with the gift of a rifle. It was not hard to imagine a boy, in shades of gray, sitting at a counter at the Stanley Club restaurant, waiting for Corinna's shift to end. And I could see all those things covered by years, marked only by a small fading scar in a tree trunk.

We checked some traps and collected the drowned animals caught in them and threw their bodies in the back of the Jeep. We drove toward Stanley in near darkness. Little bits of frost fell through the beams of our headlights. I held the loaded .257 between my knees, waiting for a deer in the road, as there was still room in the freezer for another one, and we both believed that killing one this late in the year could be an act of salvation, because things out there sometimes starved to death before spring.

I'm in a checkout line at a Salt Lake City mall. I'm behind a woman who tells the clerk she's buying a gift for her twenty-five-year-old daughter. The clerk responds that she can't believe the woman is old enough to have a child of twenty-five.

"I'm forty-two," says the woman.

There are several small children hanging on to the woman's skirt and the clerk, now aware of her advanced age, asks if she's babysitting grandchildren.

"No," she says. "They're mine. I have twelve altogether. But I do have eight grandchildren."

She speaks with pride and she turns to me, beaming.

I beam back at her, grateful for her fecundity.

I had driven to Salt Lake from Ely, Nevada, through the desert mountains west of Delta, Utah. It's a long and empty drive, through piles of sunbaked liver-colored rock and the stunted brush of dry gulches. It doesn't look as if anything bigger than a jackrabbit can live out there. A shadowy rectangle on the map indicates that just north of the highway is the Dugway Proving Grounds, which is where they tested nerve gas during the Cold War. After eighty or a hundred miles of bitterbrush and sand, when you haven't passed a car or a house or a cow, you begin to think that if they had to test nerve gas, Dugway was as good a location as any.

And people are still playing with nerve gas there. While I was driving that long lonesome road, the Delta AM station reported, between episodes of Rush Limbaugh, that two Dugway chemists had been disciplined for not reporting a lab accident involving a small atmospheric release of sarin, a nerve gas that causes profuse sweating, nausea, dry mouth, and other uncomfortable symptoms at low doses. A high dose causes death. That's how you tell if it's a high dose.

I'm not sure what the two chemists were up to. It could have been one more instance of sick laboratory humor brought on by too many years in the desert in a windowless building with Rush Limbaugh on the radio for three hours a day. I started thinking about what it might be like to be one of those chemists, whose job it must be to find peacetime uses for sarin. Sarin Wrap, maybe. Sarin Dippity Styling Gel. Sarin-Ade—the Sports Drink for the Opposing Team.

It would not be a good life, I decided. Here you are, working eight hours a day, five days a week, fifty weeks a year, with stuff that causes agony and death when any creature with a nervous system breathes it in. You may not want to imagine the nature of the experiments with sarin, unless you have the laboratory-dog franchise for Utah.

And outside, the scenery looks as though it's been burnt and then somebody collected the ashes and burnt them. The mountains are miles away, and the empty space between you and them threatens to suck out your soul and scatter it, in small pieces, over the salt pans and alkali flats. And Limbaugh on the radio, reminding you of every playground bully you ever skipped recess to avoid, telling you the real enemy isn't Chinese naval strength. It's closer, he's saying, right here at home, in the form of neighbors or family members who voted for liberals.

This is the way the world could end, I thought. Somebody at the lab could start sneaking little flasks of sarin out in his lunch bucket, just to have something to wave under the nose of a world too big and too bullying and too full of betrayal.

But now, the woman with twenty descendants is ahead of me in the checkout line and she takes my mind away from the emptiness I've just driven through. I begin to think of the holiday season ahead and of a houseful of happy children, of presents and laughter and the saying of grace around a great table laden with turkey and pumpkin pies and sweet potatoes. I think of board games and toy trains and the gentle drone of avuncular football announcers describing playoff hits. It is not just the promise of a solvent Social Security fund that makes me smile benignly at the woman's large and permanently maternal shape. She is life in a world of wind-whipped space and governments who research death and talk-show hosts who preach civil war.

It isn't until after I get back on the Interstate and am near the Idaho border that I realize how odd my reaction to this woman has been. Normally when I hear of people with twelve children, or even five or six, I think of Bangladesh or Calcutta or Nairobi. I remember that within human history, forests grew in the Sahara. I remember that I've said those places are what the whole world will be like, and soon, if people don't quit breeding like bunnies. I've been worried about overpopulation ever since I figured out how to use the multiplication function on a pocket calculator.

But there for a moment, in Utah, I had a different idea. The drive from Ely to Delta had shown me, outside the thin glass of the windshield, something alien and species-threatening.

In Idaho, amid the faint green of new winter wheat, I start to think that deserts that won't grow grass will still grow religion. Deserts let you hear the voices in whirlwinds, and those voices speak of beginnings and endings. For a few of them, the beginning was the Word and the end has much to do with wars and rumors of wars, with fire mingled with blood and with the mystery of God being finished.

It's all there in Revelation, which ends on a high note, but not before the green grass and a third part of the trees have been burnt up, a third part of the sea has turned to blood, plagues have visited humankind, and people have sought death but not found it. Where land is green, these prophecies seem unlikely, but out there in the Utah desert they've already happened. It's the end of the world. Go check it out, if you need a reason to go forth and multiply.

In the parking lot of the McDonald's on Blue Lakes Boulevard in Twin Falls, Idaho, I realize how the guy who works out at Dugway manages to keep from going completely crazy. He's married to the mega-mom in the checkout line at the mall.

Every day after work he goes home and opens the door to her and a houseful of children and grandchildren, on chaotic, diaper-reeking, howling, screaming, laughing life, and that moment is the antidote to his job, his radio program, and the metallic chill the desert blows through his soul when he looks through the mesh of the Cyclone fence. On bad days, I think, he decides to have another child.

History, before it ends, may record that an excess of humans *were driven into desert areas to work on defense projects involving weapons of mass destruction. This phenomenon strengthened apocalyptic religions that encouraged more humans to have more offspring, which ultimately produced more deserts and gave rise to more defense projects, and so on and so on until the gods, thoroughly disturbed by the way their experiment was going, rang down the curtain on the whole shooting match.*

Some Fish Stories

F OR FIFTEEN SUMMERS my father guided his clients
up and down the banks of the Salmon River near our
ranch in Sawtooth Valley, charging them $10 a day and
guaranteeing them a Chinook salmon on the line.

Among his clients was presidential adviser Sherman
Adams, of vicuña coat fame, who had come to Idaho to find
a location for a Western Camp David. Eisenhower wanted a
place in the Rockies, and Adams, detailed to search out the
perfect spot, had chosen Redfish Lake, probably on a morning when he and my father were reeling in big fish where
its outlet hits the Salmon River. Then Eisenhower had his
heart attack, and his doctors wouldn't allow him much above
sea level. Redfish Lake as a presidential retreat was finished.

Shortly after Eisenhower's heart attack, Adams accepted
that coat from a lobbyist and was forced to resign in the en-
suing scandal. He didn't go fishing with my father again, and
I suppose he must have seen the connection between the big

struggling salmon he had reeled in—so close to their destination when they took the bait—and his own fall from grace. Where once there had been clear mountain mornings, the singing of taut line against the current, the shake of great green heads against the hook, now lay only deadly metaphor.

It was in July of a year when the water was high. My father had a client who was a psychoanalyst from New York. They were fishing a hole that was lined with willows on their side of the river, and casting a line out was difficult. There was open bank on the other side, and the analyst said it appeared that they should wade across.

My father shook his head. "The river's bigger than it looks," he said. "You can't wade across it this time of year."

A momentary shift in the analyst's eyes made my father realize that the man thought he was lying.

My father went back to trying to get a fish on the line. Out in the deep current, behind a large rock, he could see the shapes of three salmon, two females and a jack. He cast out once, then again, then watched his cluster of eggs eddy around the rock, and watched the jack take it. He set the hook.

When he looked down the river, all he saw sticking out of the water was a hand clutching a salmon rod as it was swept under a line of overhanging willow bushes. He ran down the bank, pulled his client up from deep water and willow roots and quickly had him coughing and wheezing on dry ground.

Drowning, in this instance, was one of the occupational hazards of psychoanalysis. Here was a man who had spent his life trying to get his patients to take the terrible metaphors of their lives less literally. But he was faced with a literal river, which he insisted on seeing as a metaphor. He would have drowned in his metaphor if my father hadn't been literal-minded enough to run down and pull him out.

When my father tells the story, that's the end of it. When I tell the story, I wonder what happened to his pole and the jack salmon that swam, hooked deep, at the end of his line.

A family—a lawyer, and his wife, and their two sons, one in college and the other a senior in high school—showed up at the usual time, four in the morning, for my mother's sour-dough pancakes and black coffee. They all planned on going out on the river and fishing at first light. It was cold that morning and there was frost on the ground even though it was the middle of July. The woman looked around our kitchen, at the old rocking chairs in the living room, at the teakettle steaming on the woodstove, and at my mother, comfortable and happy in the middle of it.

"You men can go fishing," the woman told the rest of her family. She looked at my mother. "If it's all right, I'll stay here with you." It was my mother's custom to go back to bed after she had fixed my father and his clients breakfast, but she said she would be glad to have the company.

The men had good luck that morning. The limit then was two Chinook a day. Because salmon in a quick-running river are hard to hook if you don't know what you're doing, my father would hook one and hand the pole to the client—which is how he could guarantee a fish on the line—then take the client's pole, hook another, hand that fish off, and so on. Of course, it also took skill to land a salmon in current, so more than half of the fish got away. But by nine that morning, when the sun was just beginning to take the chill off the air, there were six big salmon lined up on the grass of our front yard.

When my father walked into the kitchen with the good news, he found the lawyer's wife crying in my mother's arms. My mother looked up at him, warning him with her expression not to let this sort of thing happen again.

All had gone well in the house until they had got on the subject of fishing. Then the lawyer's wife confessed that she was hoping that no fish would be caught that morning.

"I always root for the fish," she said. "I wish they would let them live."

My mother replied that with salmon, it wasn't a matter of living. The salmon in the backyard had made their way from the Pacific to their spawning grounds. After spawning in the wide shallows of the upper river, their bodies would quickly soften and die.

"They swim all the way up here?" asked the lawyer's wife. "Then they spawn? Then they die?"

"Yes," my mother said. "Yes."

One of my earliest memories is of being in a rowboat on Stanley Lake with my father and my uncle and fifteen or so sacks of Rotenone, a fish poison that causes death by suffocation. Their were many boats like ours on the lake. The Idaho Fish and Game Department was treating the lake, to get rid of the suckers and squawfish and freshwater herring that inhabited its bottom.

For a morning we rowed around, dragging the sacks of poison through the water, turning Stanley Lake into a kind of fish Dachau, killing not just suckers and squawfish but also the native cutthroat and Dolly Varden, and kokanee and sockeye, and the mussel beds in the outlet and down Valley Creek, destroying a 10,000-year-old ecosystem in a few hours. We had brought sacks to take the dead trout home in, because the flesh of the fish was undamaged. The poison is mostly harmless if you don't have to breathe water.

I don't remember that we gathered up any fish. There may be some instinct for salvation that prevented my father and uncle from picking up the big trout that floated around our boat and taking them home for Sunday dinner.

I'm on the boat dock of the Redfish Lake Lodge, in the summer of 1957, and I'm six years old. The campgrounds around the lake haven't been developed yet, and the few columns of smoke that rise from the trees around the lake are from campfires that have been built in rings of rocks pried from the hillsides. People are still sawing down trees so they'll have places to park their camp trailers. I'm here because my father is working on the water lines between the cabins. Some of them have frozen during the winter and now that the frost is out of the ground, he's dug down to them and is welding the places where pipes have split.

It's a warm day. I have a small fishing rod, given to me for my last birthday. It's got a little reel and twenty yards of high-strength salmon line on it. At the end of the line are five or six knots that secure a heavy red-and-white painted steel spoon with a treble hook at its end.

Within a few minutes of my arrival at the end of the dock, I've managed to get my reel snarled in a great tangle of backlash. I lack the motor skills to untangle anything beyond my shoelaces, so I've quit fishing and am sitting in the sun, looking at my shoes and the lake and beyond them to the two high peaks, Mount Heyburn and the Grand Mogul, that rise from the far shore. Snow reaches from the summit of the Mogul down its north-facing couloir almost to the water. The forest is dark green below it. The sky has no clouds and is a deep blue. What little wind there is charts aimless swirls on the glassy lake surface. Even though it's July, the lake is mostly empty of boats. It's quiet. I'm happy. I don't care if I'm not going to catch anything. I'm getting a little sleepy when I see something moving in the deep water out from the dock.

It's a big sockeye salmon. His head is olive green and his body is crimson, and he's magnified by two feet of water. He's swimming toward me and he looks like the biggest, meanest Christmas decoration I've ever seen. I want him bad.

Ten feet of line still stretch unsnarled out from my reel, and I'm able to pick up my pole and cast the spoon a little way just as he gets in range. The spoon plunks down in front of his nose, and begins to sway side to side through the water, drifting down to where all he has to do to swallow it is open his mouth.

He opens his mouth. He's going to bite. But I get too excited and just before he reaches the spoon I jerk the pole as hard as I can. The spoon shoots upward, breaks the surface, arcs through the air over my head, and embeds its hook in the wood of the dock behind me.

By the time I get it free, the sockeye has made a slow circle in front of me and has headed back in the direction he came from. The slap of the spoon on the water that comes with my desperate second cast sparks a few quick moves with his tail and he's gone.

It's the last sockeye I can remember seeing in Redfish Lake. The runs lasted a while after that, until all the dams were in place, and perhaps I looked out from the shores at reddened shallows during spawning season, but I can't remember seeing them. When I knew enough to look for them, there weren't any left.

Some Idaho rivers that once had salmon but don't have any now are the Boise, the Snake, the Weiser, the Malad. Some Idaho lakes that once held spawning sockeye but don't any longer are Yellowbelly, Pettit, and Stanley. The salmon runs were destroyed by the people who built the Hell's Canyon dams. The lakes were poisoned by the Idaho Fish and Game Department and then planted with rainbow and cutthroat. The Fish and Game Department planted other lakes as well.

High lakes in the Sawtooths were planted by helicopter in the early sixties. If you make the effort to climb up to them and throw a line in the water, ancient cutthroat, the survivors of environments too rocky or too deep or too cold to reproduce in, will swim lazily to take your fly. Planted as fry, some of them are now twenty inches long. They have huge heads and bodies like snakes. They'll weigh a good half-pound.

In one lake I know of, there is only one fish left. I've caught him every time I've gone up there for the last ten years. It's like the rat experiments where they feed half-rat rations that result in double-rat lifespans: If you're a trout, and your lake is only ice-free six weeks a year, you eat a high-protein diet of bugs for those six weeks, go to sleep the rest of the time, and get to be 100 years old before you know it.

Lately I've been thinking about all the sadness that attends the death of a salmon run. I remember seeing schools of sockeye swim in Redfish waters, and I remember the spawning Chinook that were thick in the river where it runs through the pasture west of my house. Other, older, people remember when spawning salmon could be seen from Boise bridges or be speared with pitchforks in the irrigation ditches of Weiser hayfields.

One of the things that happen when we get confronted with no-fish-where-fish-used-to-be is that we remember moments when we looked with wonder at a world not entirely reduced to human dimension.

The grief that attends that memory is unbearable. That's why we pretend that the runs can be restored again, as if those restored runs would be anything but the Chinook and sockeye equivalent of planted rainbow. If we admit what has finally happened—that the wild runs are extinct—we end up like that lawyer's wife of long ago—mourning the death of the poor fish, but actually mourning the death of a wondering part of ourselves.

About the time the viable runs of sockeye at Redfish Lake ended, there was a family that used to camp up Fishhook Creek a mile or so from where it entered the lake. There was a road up there then, since blocked by the Forest Service. This family used to spear and shoot the spawning salmon and get drunk and fight and cut down green trees and paint their names on rock faces and run their World War II–surplus four-wheel drives up hillsides. Nobody bothered them much because they were scary to look at and scarier to talk to. They had an attitude that *dared* you to tell them they were doing something wrong.

After the sockeye all died and the road had been closed, they were still walking up there, this time taking out the spawning Dolly Varden with .22 rifles. I remember walking by their camp one afternoon and seeing a big Dolly, a .22 hole in her dorsal hump, trying to swim up over a broken beaver dam, too weak to swim against the center of the current. She would wash backward, circle around in the eddy below the dam, then charge weakly into the current again. I watched her do this three times before I lost the strength to watch, and hurried down the closed road to my car.

Now the Dolly Varden are mostly gone and I'm not sure what that family is going to kill next, but I'm hoping that maybe they'll start in on each other.

I don't think about them much, but when I do I wonder if their Fishhook Creek ritual really isn't their way of dealing with grief.

Not too far from my house is a small valley full of beaver dams. The ponds behind them are full of brook trout and native cutthroat, and they're hard to fish. There's a way to do it, though—and it doesn't involve firearms—and when I get hungry for fish I go up there and catch a quick half-dozen.

They're tiny. A half-dozen will make a couple of people a meal, if you've got a vegetable and a dessert. But they haven't come out of a fish truck and they recall other times, other fish.

The biggest fish I ever caught wasn't a fish at all. It was a baby beluga whale, pale white and drowned, hanging in the nets of a gillnetter I worked on in Bristol Bay in Alaska. It had struggled and broken the net in some places, but in others the net had held and had cut deep into the whale's skin. It was a scene of surpassing cruelty. I pulled the nets one way and then another, and the whale gradually untangled, rolled to the edge of the net, and sank out of sight.

A few miles above Lowman, Idaho, the South Fork of the Payette River plunges over a low falls and into a long and deep pool. Dive into that pool, swim to the eddy that swirls under the falls, and you float around and around, buoyed by a galaxy of bubbles. Swim into the current and you're swept past polished rock walls into a wide green fan of still water, where you can drop your feet to the bottom and walk out for another go-round.

And that's not the best of it. Cascading into the South Fork at just that spot are the dozen or so streams and pools of Kirkham Hot Springs. If you're chilled by the river you can stoop under a hot waterfall or sit in one of the pools until your body temperature gets back up to where the river seems nicely cold.

While Kirkham is a seductive place, it is not pristine. There's a campground there, and across the river is Highway 21 and a bar/café/store/gas station, partially scorched and partially rebuilt after the '89 fire. People bring their coolers and their kids down to the river's edge and you watch this spread-out amphibious thing with six or eight mouths gorge itself on potato salad and chicken parts and Pepsi. Garbage is tossed into the river, running shoes float out of sight, and sometimes there are used disposable diapers steaming on the asphalt of the parking lot.

None of which matters much as you jump off the rocks on the highway side of the river, fall through ten feet of air to the water, and sink down and down through the bubbles. If you wear goggles, you'll find that the bubbles end halfway to the bottom, and you can see the whole wet length of the hole under a foamy ceiling. Car parts and fishing lures litter the bottom. A distant light flashes off the fish scales, broken glass, and crumples of foil. It takes little imagination to discover your childhood down there too, unbroken, unaged, and uncorroded as an aluminum beer can. Sometimes you get out of the water substantially younger than when you jumped into it.

As is my habit, I spent parts of last summer at Kirkham, usually when a planned trip to the Boise Towne Square Mall lost its appeal in the face of more immediate pleasures. The faded shopping lists lying about my car may wait until Lowman gets an enclosed shopping environment of its own.

I spent long afternoons on the riverside rocks, watching the water and the families, choosing hot water or cold depending on the arrangement of clouds and sun. Worries of global warming catastrophes, nerve gas, and subcutaneous tracking devices were replaced by a conviction that the gods were in a generous mood and were being particularly generous with me.

That bliss lasted into August, but in the middle of that month I began noticing single mothers on the bank beside me, single mothers with weary and worried eyes, whose voices were harsh from yelling at children.

"Don't jump off that rock!" they would yell.

Small children on the other side of the river would look at them curiously, cup their hands to their ears, shrug, and jump off the rock into the water. A minute or two later they would float to the surface and paddle toward us.

"We're never coming here again," the mothers would yell, but neither the children, nor I, nor the mothers themselves believed it. I'd see the same people in the same ritual a week or two later.

Self-consciousness slid into my afternoons like a snake into a garden. I'd seen these women before, women with too many kids and not enough money, in all our fine Idaho places where admission isn't charged: on the beach at Redfish Lake, in the unimproved campgrounds along the Salmon River, on the trails to the low-lying lakes of the Sawtooths. Their eyes were weary from raising kids alone and worried because child-support checks had not always come when they should have and moral support had stopped coming at all. I began to joke that one could serve humanity well by sitting with wrenches and screwdrivers in the picnic area at Redfish Lake and fixing the bikes of children whose fathers weren't there. But the joke wasn't funny. It was simply sad and true.

Back at Kirkham, I began to see half-families everywhere I looked. And no longer were they objects of mild amusement. Families fragment into painfully vulnerable people. It was through their vulnerable eyes that I saw myself as a grown man acting like a joyous ten-year-old, spending his peak-earning summers jumping off rocks into rivers, being at least as irresponsible as ex-spouses had been in their most irresponsible moments. You could die at Kirkham, I saw, not by getting snagged on an old Chevrolet door handle jammed between bottom rocks, but by being stoned by a mob of single working mothers who recognized in you that same instinct for old pleasure that had made other men run to new states, new jobs, and new women.

The last few times I've been in the pools, school has been in ses-sion. There's a fee box in the parking lot now, and you're supposed to pay $3 to park your car there. Aside from a few local Forest Ser-vice workers and a couple of unemployed flight attendants, I've had the place to myself.

It's just as well. If you're half smart, you don't try to reassure the children of strangers that the same river can be jumped into, again and again, for all of a life. They would have already been warned about people like me, who smile at them and tell them things they've already seen aren't true.

Solo

IN MAY 1967 I moved into a small log cabin in the center of Stanley, just across the alley from the Stanley Club. When I moved in, the cabin had no toilet or shower or hot water. There was an outhouse out back and a washroom with a bathtub and a sink. When I needed a bath, I filled the bathtub with buckets of water I heated on the woodstove. The roof leaked in a dozen places, and I spent three days nailing down a new tar-paper roof before I unpacked.

My landlord was an old friend of my parents named Russell Vaughan, who with his wife, Susie, had run a small restaurant and saddle shop and the local state liquor store out of the cabin during the fifties and early sixties. Russ had been in the U.S. Cavalry when it was still mostly horse-mounted, and after that had trained as an undertaker. He had practiced his trade for only a few years in Chicago before striking out for the West and less gloomy occupations. He and Susie had come into the country as caretakers for the mines at Seafoam, forty miles west of Stanley, during the thirties. Their home had been one of the places where my father had found refuge when he ran away from his own family at age fourteen. When the mines had closed, Russ and Susie had invested their life savings in a half-block of Stanley. Susie was a licensed practical nurse, and for many years the state liquor store was also the valley's more-or-less free medical clinic.

By 1967 Susie had been dead of lung cancer for three years. Russ was living month to month on Social Security, crippled with emphysema, and had gone a little crazy with grief and loneliness. My parents visited him often, but my father had begun working on road construction in other parts of Idaho and they were only in the valley on weekends.

Russ had offered to rent the cabin to me and I had decided to live there with what I thought was a high-school graduate's complete independence. But the arrangement had undoubtedly been concluded between Russ and my parents, as a way of keeping an eye on me during that dangerous time while I decided between college and war—and also as a way of making sure Russ had company.

His home was next door to my cabin. On most sunny summer days I would see him on his front porch. He would sit motionless, silently and sadly watching the tourists drive up and down the dusty streets. What he saw when he looked at them was not what I saw. A flash of fender, a face behind a car window, a waved arm, a license plate from a state with an ocean—I sensed that these were doorways to the past for him and it appeared that he spent most of his time on their thresholds.

That June Russ purchased a metal detector and after

work I would go with him to nearby gulches and glades where he said cabins had once been standing, and we would hunt for lost silver and gold or, failing that, what we called antiques. At his direction I dug up old wagon axles, Model-T engine blocks, iron water pipes, harness buckles, rotting singletrees, fragments of antique roofing tin, and hundreds upon hundreds of antique bottle caps and rusted antique cans. When my father found out what we were doing, he told me that most people who had lived in those cabins in Sawtooth Valley hadn't had much money and had kept track of what they did have well enough that Russ and I weren't going to get rich off what they had lost. But we persisted.

Occasionally, I dug up something that could be classed as a real antique, a sun-tinted bottle or a finely blacksmithed wagon step and once an ornate cast-iron cigar cutter, its blade rusted and dull. When I unearthed the cigar cutter, Russ looked at it and said, "That's not an antique. We had those when I was a kid." He found this idea amusing. After that, whenever I went with him to the Stanley Club café for a hamburger, he would point to the antiques hanging on its walls and tell the teenage waitresses the same thing, and grin, and then wait long moments for them to laugh.

I worked on the plumbing of both the cabin and Russ's house, following his instructions. We went to Boise with $100 I had received as a graduation gift and came home with a used water heater, a shower stall, and a toilet, which I installed in the back room of the cabin, once again with his guidance and under the impression that I was the one helping him out.

One day toward the end of that summer he told me to get the ladder that hung on the side of his house and move it to his front porch. He had an old cow skull that he had found on one of our metal-detecting expeditions, and he had painted these words on its forehead: "Wagon bustid. Water gon. Horses ded. Indians. 5 bullits left. *Russ.*" He had me nail the skull onto the gable end above his front porch. Another time I found him in his kitchen, filing two notches in the butt of the Colt service revolver he had been issued during his time in the army. He had a subscription to a wild-west magazine called *True Frontier,* and I wondered at the time if he was taking its articles too seriously. But in the hills around Stanley he had showed me several places where he claimed bodies had been buried. I didn't have the presence of mind, much less the courage, to ask him if they had anything to do with the notches he was filing on the revolver.

During that and subsequent winters Russ moved out of Stanley. One more January without decent TV would kill him, he said. He owned a small house trailer and he parked it in the backyard of my family's house in Hailey. I remember coming home from college during Christmas vacation of 1972 and finding him noticeably frailer. He was having difficulty breathing. My parents took care of him in their house when he became bedridden. A month later they took him to the Veterans' Hospital in Boise, and he died there in the early spring.

He gave the cabin to me and his house and land to my parents. Not long after he died, the Stanley Club burned down. I was back at college, and the only thing that kept my cabin from burning was the Highway Department's rotary snowplow, which moved down the unplowed alley through drifts six feet high, covering the cabin's smoking walls with a layer of snow. When Russ died my father called to tell me the news after the funeral was over. When the Stanley Club burned, he told me that it had been a near thing, but that the fire was out and my cabin was still standing. Listening, homesick and helpless at the faraway end of a phone line, I had the sensation both times that my emotional center was not my own, that it belonged instead to things already in the past: the lives, the deaths, the carelessness or kindness of other people.

During one fall, my parents lived in the house Russ had given them, but after that they rented it out until one of their renters burned it down in 1986. I only lived in my cabin during the summers, but it was the place I called home until I built my house on the Salmon River.

One of Russ's stories was of a winter in the early fifties when it got to sixty-three below zero Fahrenheit in town.

A teacher from Georgia had been hired that fall for the elementary school and had announced that Stanley was the most beautiful place on earth and that she planned on living there forever. She bought a pair of overshoes that Russ described as coming up to her ankles and a heavy winter coat. She lived in the teacherage next to the school, which was insulated and had a huge oil stove for heat, but when the cold hit that winter, she put on her overshoes and winter coat and waded through two feet of snow to the mailman's car. He took her to Ketchum, where she got on a train for Georgia, even though the teacherage's pipes hadn't frozen as they had in most of the houses in town. She never returned.

Another effect of the record cold was that a case of crème de menthe that Russ had in the liquor store turned from a deep green to a bright pink, and it didn't turn back to green once it warmed up. I have no idea what chemistry was involved in the change, but I've had trouble drinking anything green since.

In 1981 I was driving home from Missoula, Montana, on December 10, and stopped at a restaurant in Salmon, Idaho, 100 miles downriver from Stanley. The temperature-and-time sign on a nearby bank was alternately flashing 4:00 P.M. and 55° F.

I had drained the water from my cabin a month earlier, but I camped there for the night, building a fire in the stove and throwing a sleeping bag on the bed. The next morning I woke up at six, freezing. It was fifty-five below zero. A hundred miles and fourteen hours had produced a temperature change of a hundred and ten degrees. A family that had built a big new log house on the outskirts of town were huddled in blankets around the big oil stove in the hotel. The children were big-eyed and teary, the wife silent, and the husband worried and staring uncomprehendingly out of the window at their home. Their pipes had frozen and they couldn't get their high-ceilinged living room above forty degrees, and from the looks of things, the marriage wouldn't get above freezing until summer. At 4:00 P.M. that day someone was towing a new Chevrolet Blazer down Main Street, trying to get it started. All four wheels were locked up and it was making shallow trenches with its tires as it was dragged down the packed snow. A cold gray cloud of ice hovered above the roofs of town, obscuring the peaks and turning every color in town shadowy. On that day, I had no trouble believing that another winter day had been eight degrees cooler.

. . .

Even with a box in the Stanley post office and more time in residence than most of the people in town, I remember feeling like an outsider most of the time I was there.

I'm still not a local. A few years ago, Jasper LiCalzi, a political science professor from Philadelphia who teaches with me at Albertson College, drove into Stanley looking for me. I had told him I lived in Stanley.

He stopped at the Chevron station in town and asked where my house was.

The woman at the counter shrugged.

"You know him?" asked Jasper.

"I know of him," said the woman. "He's kind of a hippie. Did he tell you he lived in Stanley?"

"How small does a town have to get before you know where people live in it?" asked Jasper. "Twenty people? Ten?"

"He doesn't live in Stanley," said the woman.

"Where does he live?"

"Up the valley somewhere," said the woman.

Jasper finally found someone willing to give him directions to my house, but that person, too, emphasized that I didn't live in Stanley and said that I had been misleading him when I said I did. Later that afternoon, as we sat on my deck drinking beer and watching a warm sun tint the Sawtooths orange and red and pink, I explained to Jasper that to be a true resident of Stanley you had to pay your dues.

I had learned of this requirement one early April, when I had put the water back in my cabin, shoveled a tunnel through the pile of snow the town plow had put at my front door, and moved in for the summer. After mopping and cleaning windows and lighting the water heater, I went down to John and Mary's, which had lately become the Kasino Club, for a burger.

The person sitting beside me at the bar was new to me. I introduced myself, and he said his name was Tom. I said I had moved up for the summer. He looked at me, snorted contempt, and informed me that people who only lived in Stanley in the summer were called summer people. I liked that. It was logical, and it was better than being called a hippie.

"Yes," I said. "Summer people."

I had just spent the winter on the ski patrol in Sun Valley. My job as a wilderness ranger with the Forest Service wouldn't start for two months, and I had my first unemployment check of the year in my pocket. In spite of my heavy winter clothes and the roof-high mound of snow on my doorstep, it felt like summer to me.

"You're not a local," he said.

"Summer person," I said.

"I'm a local," he said. He was a young man, but he was leaning over his beer like a half-uprooted tree and had the same aura of irreparable damage. He told me he had come to town late last fall and was planning on living in Stanley forever. He had rented a place in town and had lived there with his dog for the winter. In six weeks he would start a job as a river guide.

"If you want to be a local in this town, you've got to pay your dues," he said. "You can't just waltz in when the weather gets warm and act like you own the place."

It was six winters before he left town. He was a skier, which helps if you're trying to get through December, January, and February here. He painted and did carpentry and made enough to get from one tourist season to the next.

As it happened, he became the renter who burned Russ's house down. It was another April when he went out on the Salmon River for an early float with some friends. They had drunk beer all day while floating in water that flowed through banks lined with ice. He had come back to Russ's house, chilled to the bone and stumbling, and had built a great fire in the woodstove and gone to sleep on the couch. When he woke up it was because of the shouts of people who were trying to determine if anyone was still alive in a house that was blowing flame from every window. He crawled to safety in the eight inches of breathable air above the floor. His old dog didn't make it out.

He disappeared for a week but finally called my parents, who explained to him that the house had been insured and that what had happened was the reason they had insurance in the first place. He came back to town, but he didn't make it through another winter. By January the locals started calling him Tom the Torch, and the fire was what they wanted to talk about when he went to the bar. He finally went away and became a local somewhere else.

I explained all this to Jasper, but then, because he's a person who is interested in communities and the shadows they cast, I went further and tried to explain why you couldn't tell someone who lived in Stanley that you lived in Stanley, even if you did live there. It was safer just to assume outsider status from the beginning, because it was where you would end up.

"To start with, Stanley people aren't tourists. Everybody goes along with that, even the tourists, who will come right out and tell you they're on vacation and don't really belong here.

"Then there are the people who stay through the winter and the people who don't. In the winter, there are the people who have jobs and the people on unemployment. The people who drink in the bars and the people who drink alone. The people who have a sexual partner and the single males. Regular people and what in Stanley are still known as hippies. The people who have good luck and the people, like Tom the Torch, who don't. The people who have been here long enough and the people who haven't. By the end of the winter, the divisions have gotten down to dietary habits and rumored sexual tastes and almost everyone in Stanley thinks everyone else is an outsider. It's a lonely town by March."

"Fifty years isn't long enough to be a local?" asked Jasper.

"Not if you're a summer person," I said. "Or a hippie."

"I don't get why this is important."

"That's why you'll never be a local."

But lots of people do want to be locals in Stanley. Come in from Boise on a June evening when the sun has come out after a thunderstorm and you'll see why. The town lies golden in cloud-mirrored light in the center of green fields full of elk and cattle. Hawks scream high and clear and wild above roadside turnouts. Calves butt heads on the other side of log fences from the highways. Sandhill cranes fly up and down Valley Creek, their loud mutterings echoing off the creek-side cliffs. Willow and aspen show bits of neon leaf along their branches. Water, blue and white, overflows the creek banks and chokes the swirling mouths of culverts. Above the town, the Sawtooths rise 4,000 feet, snow-covered where the rock isn't vertical. The new summer subdivisions of the past fifteen years only detract a little from this vision.

Tourists in stiff new blue jeans will be walking the dirt streets of town. Winnebagos and bicycles will be trundling back and forth between Stanley and Redfish Lake. In the Rod and Gun Club, young men from Los Angeles and Seattle and Boise will be teaching young women from New York and Denver and Pocatello how to swing dance. Newly hired river guides will be strutting around town as though they own the place.

None of these people will be locals, but many of them will be dreaming of ways to become one, and some of them, possessed by near-religious visions of homesteading in a small and historyless town in a green and glorious corner of the earth, will find a way to not go home in the fall. That dreams are indifferent to and more enduring than the human material they use to enact themselves is not something they're thinking about. They're not thinking of where those dreams came from or what they might put a person through or how much they might cost that person's loved ones.

Some of them will last until the real cold hits in December. Some of them, usually people who have learned to back-country ski, will make it all the way through the winter, having discovered a different kind of glory in the ice and snow of the Sawtooths, and they'll stay as athletes, mountain climbing, kayaking, and skiing as long as their college loans and deferred careers can stand it.

Occasionally a young couple with some money saved up

will put a down payment on a lot and go away to jobs that will sustain the payments on it for twenty years. Usually only one of them makes it back, because land in a suburb of Stanley, if you're planning on building on it someday, takes the dream-energy that could help sustain a marriage. Sometimes one of them will get the lot as the spoils of a divorce, and it has happened that those small pieces of land have become the centerpieces of new courtships.

Even the wonderfully wealthy that are an increasing part of Stanley's suburban population seldom stay for more than a few seasons. They build estates full of ponds, fences, and log houses and even tennis courts. For a while they live on them, but after a winter most of them move down to Sun Valley. They grow old, they grow bored, and they go south, and their hardheaded children sell out to other, even wealthier dreamers, who see themselves at the mere beginnings of forever.

The first memory I have of Stanley is of the Rod and Gun Club burning down. I was four, too young for school, and I remember walking through its still-smoking foundations a few days after the fire, staring in wonder at melted whisky bottles, skeletal slot machines, and the labyrinth of basement corridors suddenly exposed to sunlight. My parents must have been visiting Russ and Susie and I must have wandered off. It must have caused some worry, because they all came looking for me at once.

When they found me I was clutching a burnt metal bucket full of big souvenir nails and half-collapsed bottles. My face and arms and legs were black with soot and my hair was full of ashes. I was pulled out of the ruins and given a bath and told never to go there again. There were still hot spots there, places where thick buried logs were burning, hollowing out caves that could collapse if you walked above them. One minute I could have been on solid ground and the next found myself deep in the earth with my bones being eaten up by red coals and flickering flames. That was the way Susie explained it to me—her background had been Southern Baptist and she came by those images honestly.

According to what Russ told me many years later, the Rod and Gun was rebuilt in time for it to be open the next summer and sold as usual the following fall. The owner at that time had the place perennially for sale. He sold it every September, getting a modest down payment, offering easy terms and keeping the paper.

The payments always stopped coming. The new owners would usually clear out in February, leaving water in the pipes, which would then break and flood the basement halfway to the floorboards. The old owner would foreclose and go back in April, replumb the place, melt the ice out of the basement with a space heater, restock the liquor, hire a cook, and run it for another summer. The place was profitable in July and August and broke even in the fall when the hunters came down from the hills to drink. The old owner made a living on down payments until he found a cash buyer and retired in 1967, having made a success of a tough business in a difficult climate.

Russ had a story about one of these new owners, a good-hearted and friendly man who, after making his down payment in September, began making preparations to keep the place profitable all winter. He began stacking firewood on the sidewalk out in front of the bar in early October.

He had decided that keeping a constant roaring fire in the big fireplace would make the Rod and Gun a pleasant, warm spot for his new neighbors to do their drinking. He had never run a bar before, but thought that if you could make a place where people would feel at home and be able to drink with their friends in a convivial atmosphere, you would provide solace for the lonely and good cheer for the depressed, and make your payments in the bargain. He even built library shelves near the fireplace and filled them with a well-thumbed collection of self-help and get-rich-quick books.

He had not reckoned with Stanley in the winter or the people who lived there. In his quest for firewood that October, he had cut down a big dead tree on the road to Stanley Lake. It was 400 years old and had finally perished a couple of years earlier from old age, drought, insects, and lightning strikes. It was right next to the road and was a hazard to everyone who drove by, and the Forest Service would have had to cut it down anyway if no one had done it for them.

That fact didn't matter much to many of the locals, who took it upon themselves to designate the fallen tree as a lost landmark and the new owner of the Rod and Gun as an interloper and newcomer who had no respect for community tradition. The rest of the people in town were angry because they had missed out on that much firewood that close to the road.

People started to refer to the tree as the Old Man, although I had never heard it called anything in particular when it was still standing. Cut up into blocks and stacked, the Old Man became a log wall that obscured the Rod and Gun's front windows. The larger blocks were fifty inches across, and had to be split with a sledgehammer and wedges. The new owner would buy you a beer if you split one of them into small pieces, but that turned out to be a bad deal for you unless you had no money at all.

By late November, business was as grim as usual, but the new owner was undeterred. The Old Man had been split into fireplace-sized pieces, smoke roared out of the Rod and Gun's chimney every evening, and there was free chili if you showed up when it got dark and cold at 4:30 P.M. Sometimes people showed up for the chili but didn't drink anything, and some of the people who were regular drinkers left when the chili eaters showed up, lest it be thought that they couldn't pay for a meal.

The new owner's last public-spirited gesture had come in early December, when he loaded his chain saw in his four-wheel-drive pickup, drove out to Iron Creek, and came back with a twenty-foot spruce tree. He built a stand for it out of two-by-sixes, and carried it to the intersection next to the post office. He hung up a dozen red glass balls he'd found in the basement of the Rod and Gun and carefully covered the tree with a half-dozen boxes of tinsel. He bought strings of Christmas lights, strung them around and through the spruce branches, and got them burning with linked extension cords that led through a small window in the Rod and Gun to a power outlet in its restroom. At the top he put a plastic angel.

The first problem came when the local forest ranger called and told him they had had a complaint that he was cutting green timber without a permit. He explained that it was a Christmas tree for the town, which made it all right with the ranger. It didn't make it all right with those townspeople who were offended that there was an official tree in town when nobody had asked them about it. The new owner got anonymous calls about waltzing into town and acting like he owned the place.

People who had shown no previous interest in constitutional scholarship began to voice concerns about the separation of church and state. A number of the local hippies who had declared themselves pagans said they didn't want a Christian icon in the middle of Main Street. They stopped complaining as soon as they were assured that Christmas trees were pagan icons, but at that point the Christians got worried about it. There were complaints that the tree would interfere with snow removal, even after the man who ran the city plow said he could plow around it.

The people who didn't like the tree formed into one faction who refused to drink in the Rod and Gun. Many of those in the other faction were people still mourning the loss of the Old Man and they wouldn't drink there either. People who sat by the fire and grabbed a self-help or get-rich book to read started feeling guilty and poor and swore off alcohol, or at least alcohol in public. By the middle of December, paying customers had dwindled to the occasional lost traveler who came in to ask directions to Missoula after turning the wrong way and finding out that Highway 21 was closed for the winter.

It must have been a difficult epiphany. One night a week before Christmas, the new owner sat alone behind the bar, drinking up his profits, and listening to the steady throb of the oil furnace once the temperature got below zero Fahrenheit. The fireplace sucked cold air in through every crack in a window frame and every gap between the logs. Below twenty below, unless you camped right in front of the flames, throwing another log on the fire just made you colder.

He must have looked at his balance sheets and his hopes and seen that they weren't matching up. He must have heard, by that time, of the fate of other hopeful owners of his bar, and he must have gone from being a bar owner to an ex–bar owner in a second or two as the realization hit him that he wasn't going to be different from the rest. He might not have even moved. There might have been a little twitch of his eyebrows or a tap of his ring against the top of the bar.

But then he got up, put his coat on, walked out of the bar, and fired up his pickup. It was a new pickup with good tires and a plug-in headbolt heater so that it would always start in the cold. It had a toolbox in the back that held a chain saw, wrenches, socket sets, and logging chains in case he ever found somebody stuck in a ditch and needed to pull them out. It was a pickup that was prepared for anything and it had been part of a dream of living in Stanley forever.

By midnight he had backed the truck up to the Christmas tree. By the light of its green, red, yellow, and blue bulbs, he hooked the log chain from the pickup's rear hitch to the bottom of the trunk, got back in the cab, and took off for the city dump. The tree bounced behind him, scattering glass and tinsel all the way out Highway 21, making the road surface look unusually festive. It was an indication of how good-hearted he was that he drained the pipes of the Rod and Gun before he turned off the oil furnace and left town for good, going back to a home and a wife no one even knew he had.

In Russ's story, the next day the man who plowed out the dump road nailed the tree's broken base back together, pushed it upright with his loader, and lifted it up on a snow-pile. Bits of bright glass and tinsel still gleamed among its branches. The angel had survived the journey, and on Christmas Day of that year its beneficent plastic grin beamed down on the smoking garbage pit of the Stanley town dump, giving the place a kind of manic cheer.

That was a long time ago. Stanley has changed. When I pick up my mail in Stanley now, I go to the new post office, across the street from where the old one was. Its parking lot is where the Ace of Diamonds used to stand, and the old building shimmers in my mind's eye, its outlines enclosing the new SUVs and convertibles and the pickups of the river runners. Stanley has become the takeoff point for float trips on the Middle Fork of the Salmon, and the people who own river companies are part of our summer population. Their warehouses and offices take up a good portion of the newly developed real estate.

A new, windowless elementary school has been built on the hill above town. The Stanley Club has become the Mountain Village Saloon and has moved east to the intersection of the two highways, part of a grocery store–gas station–motel complex that the casino magnate Bill Harrah put together before he died. The Kasino Club contains an excellent gourmet restaurant, with an international menu. There's a bakery-and-coffee shop, a mountain-and-watersports shop, and a photo gallery. Stanley is part of the

Recreational West now, and there's more money in town. The Rod and Gun hasn't changed hands for years.

In spite of these changes, or because of them, it's easier for me to understand what Russell Vaughan saw when he sat on his front porch and looked down Stanley's streets. I've lived long enough to know that you can not only sit on the threshold to the past, you can stand up and walk into it, sun yourself in its distant light, make a pallet on the floor of its empty, evanescent houses, and sleep there through its warm nights. I hope that was what Russ was doing then, and I hope that's what he's doing now.

Fifteen miles west of Stanley, Idaho, just after Highway 21 crosses Thatcher Creek, is a log-worm fence that is past its prime. The once regular zigzag of its line is broken by skewed and decayed top logs and by the hasty repairs of people more interested in keeping cattle pastured than fences aesthetic. Its panels sag and the short base logs under the zigs and the zags have rotted and sunk deep into the meadow.

The fence is made up of 1,106 sixteen-foot panels, each of them consisting of four logs, notched and interwoven with the ends of adjoining panels. It is 2.1 miles in length. The logs for its construction came from the forest that once stood where Highway 21 now sits. It was constructed at a price of $6.30 per panel, begun and finished in the summer of 1964.

I know this because I helped build it. My father had the contract for it the summer I was thirteen years old, and I got put to work doing whatever a thirteen-year-old could do on a fence job.

Base logs had to be lined out along the survey stakes. The still-

green trees from the Highway 21 right-of-way had been felled and pushed with a bulldozer into great jumbled mounds, and they had to be limbed, measured, and cut to length. Sixteen-foot logs had to be lifted onto a trailer and then laid out along the fence line in groups of four.

The work was hard and, to a thirteen-year-old, unending. My parents had put a small house trailer on the banks of Thatcher Creek and that was the family home all that summer. My bedroom was a motorcycle tent in a 1,000-acre meadow.

I wrestled base logs into place and learned to tow the trailer with the pickup while my father and his hired man scattered logs. I got better at handling green timber. I learned to use a chain saw.

Cutting logs out of great piles of dirty and frozen trees (there was ice all through the piles, even into mid-July) was dangerous work. You could slip down between tree trunks as you walked across the pile, chain saw in hand. Sometimes trees had been twisted and tensioned in the pile, and to cut them was to start a 300-pound club swinging toward your knees.

I learned to work a saw on the piles, cutting out sixteen-foot sections, tumbling them to the ground, then starting on the trees below. I measured trees, limbed them, and pried them up with a bar so that they could be sawn. Somewhere toward the end of that summer my father needed to be elsewhere on the fence, and he left me alone with a saw and a log pile.

Even now I remember being surprised at being handed the tasks of not dying, not sawing myself in half, and coming up with loads of sixteen-footers for the fence. And I remember with gratitude the wisdom that enabled my father to run down to his end of the job and leave me to mine. He gave me a gift, a lesson about living in the here and now. I may have yearned, then, for the day that the fence would be finished. But I didn't yearn for adulthood, that fabled time when a thirteen-year-old thinks he will be fully in the world. Being alone on trembling logs with a saw in my hands showed me that being fully in the world is more a function of attention than of age.

It is sobering to watch the work of my own hands fade in the sun, sag in the middle, rot, and fall apart. I drive by the old fence on my way to Boise or Kirkham Hot Springs and it is always a shock to see it. The fence in my memory is in better shape.

It would be good to think that what hasn't decayed is the knowledge of how to live in the here and now, but that knowledge, too, has faded with the years. I have trouble paying attention during the thin moment of the present. I'm no wiser than anyone else who has signed a thirty-year mortgage or spent a decade or two mourning what might have been. Now and then I yearn for adulthood.

But growing older has forced me to find value in decay. The fence that slowly sinks back toward the ground provides a metaphor for all the distinctions made between self and other, them and us, darkness and light, among past, present, and future.

Such distinctions start to weaken. Natural psychic forces, analogous to the sun, the wind, and the fungus working on old wood, begin to break them down. Both good and evil people start looking like mere human beings, subject to suffering or joy as dumb luck decrees. Loved ones or enemies begin to stare back at me with my own eyes.

And in the present, I drive past a fence and remember its once-living trees and see that hard work does come to an end. I see the creep of new lodgepole saplings from the fence line toward the frost-cracked road and know that what has come from the earth will return to the earth, if it's given time.

Making Bombs

THE SUMMER I left high school and moved into Russell Vaughn's cabin, I got a job pumping gas at the Texaco station on the highway between Upper and Lower Stanley. The job paid $2.25 an hour and allowed me to wear my first uniform, an olive-drab shirt with *Texaco* embroidered on the pocket, and black and green tie-dyed bell-bottoms—found in the sale bin of a Boise head shop—and cowboy boots, and a black felt cowboy hat with a hatband made out of aluminum pop-tops, and a pair of unclaimed aviator-style mirror-shades that had been left in the men's room. I started a goatee, let my hair grow longer than it had ever been, and looked for something to wear around my neck. I considered love beads too flashy and potentially effeminate. I finally found an old St. Christopher's medal in one of my parents' outbuildings and wore that.

One of my jobs was to clean the restrooms. The women's room had a full-length mirror on the inside of its door, and after I had swept and scoured the toilet and washbasin, I would clean the mirror, squeegee it dry, and stare for long moments at my image. I looked like no one remotely related to my history. I delighted in the thought that I had stopped being who I had been and had constructed someone else to be. There was more freedom and less fate in the world than I had been told.

My boss, who owned the station, was thirty-five, and had a wife and a new child, a mortgage, and car payments. He told me to enjoy being single while I could.

"I never knew what true happiness was until I got married," he said. "And then it was too late." It was a joke older than I was, but I'd never heard it before and I laughed until I looked up and saw that he wasn't laughing. Then he made fun of my pants and called me a hippie. Then he asked me if I could score dope for him.

The request came as a shock. I had viewed him as middle-aged and respectable. But he told me that he and his wife and another couple would go up on the hill above town, smoke fifteen or twenty joints at a time, until they couldn't move, and then they would lie back and watch the stars make brand-new constellations. He told me they did this as often as they could, but it was hard to find dope and they thought that I, as a hippie, knew where to get it.

"How much money do you need?" he asked me.

I told him I wasn't a hippie and I didn't know anybody who sold drugs and that I couldn't help him. He nodded, as though this lie that I was telling him had been expected. He said it would take a while longer before I would trust him.

· · ·

I really didn't know anybody who sold dope. My idea of serious intoxication was to buy a case of Olympia Beer and drive my brother's Mustang—left to me when he left for Vietnam—down along the Salmon River to the Saturday night dance in Challis, stand against a wall until a girl asked me to dance, and shuffle around the dance floor long enough to ask her if she wanted to go out to the car and drink beer. Usually I ended up driving back at two in the morning, drunk, listening to Glen Campbell on the eight-track, and stopping every fifteen minutes to run around the car to wake up enough to drive again.

Once, I stopped in at closing time at a Challis bar to buy a pack of No-Doz. The bartender looked at my hair and face and shook his head when I asked him if he had any.

"We got it," he said. "But I'm not selling it to you. You hippies are using it to get hopped up on."

"I'm not a hippie," I said.

By July, my goatee was beginning to look a little less like a bad case of chin fungus. There were moments, standing in front of the mirror with my shades on and the front brim of my hat pulled low, that it made me look sinister or as if I had been fighting fire. I had found another pair of bell-bottoms in another sale bin, this time with black-and-white zigzags running up and down the legs, and had bought a fringed orange leather jacket to go with them. My cowboy boots had disappeared, and in their place I wore tire-soled Mexican sandals. My boss was still asking me to score him dope.

He had given me more responsibility, letting me run the station by myself for whole days at a time. When no cars were at the pumps out front, I was in the shop, working on an 80 cc Yamaha motorcycle that was to be my first raise if I could get it running. My boss had also set me up with his wife's younger sister, who had visited for two weeks, and he had given me gas and money enough to take her to Sun Valley for pizza and a movie.

"Show her a good time," he had told me, winking, but her idea of a good time had been to read Hermann Hesse's *The Glass Bead Game* all the way over Galena Summit and to reply to my questions about her life in Los Angeles in sullen monosyllables. She criticized the pizza and said that *Five Easy Pieces* bored her and that she despised Jack Nicholson and anyone who wanted to be like Jack Nicholson. She rejected my offer to buy a six-pack of Oly. She was older than me, a sophomore at Pepperdine, a philosophy major. She read by flashlight on the way back over the summit until she got carsick. I took her home. Inside her sister's front door, four people, their twentieth joint long behind them, sat silent and unmoving in front of a TV that showed only a test pattern.

By August, the goatee was dense enough that I could see it in the dim light of the mirror in the women's restroom in the Texaco station. I was encouraged enough by its growth to attempt a mustache. My hair was almost to my shoulders. I had found a pair of tight black leather pants at a garage sale, only a little torn up where they had been in a motorcycle wreck, and had had them repaired at a saddle shop in Challis. I was wearing them most days pumping gas, along with a greasy embroidered sheepskin vest that had come from Afghanistan. At the same garage sale I had picked up a large pewter pendant cast in the shape of a peace sign and was wearing it on a leather thong around my neck, along with the Christopher medal.

One indication of my metamorphosis came from our customers. We were charging 39 cents a gallon for regular, which was a dime more than you could get it for in Boise, so it was not uncommon for a car to drive in beside the pumps, sit there until the driver noticed the price, and then drive out again. But now, cars would sit there, waiting for gas, until the drivers noticed *me*. Then they would drive off, sometimes quickly.

If my boss saw that I was losing him business he never mentioned it or asked me to change my appearance. Yet again, he asked me to buy dope for him.

"I don't know where to get it," I said.

"I thought you hippies always knew where to get it," he said.

"I'm not a hippie," I said.

"I don't know what the hell you are if you aren't," he said.

It was a time when people were doing bad things to people they mistook for hippies. Hippies, who drove around in VW vans painted in rainbow colors, who camped in teepees and swam nude in hot springs, who used illegal drugs, who wore their hair to their shoulders, who embraced nonviolence, who wouldn't work, who played Country Joe and the Fish and the Grateful Dead instead of Glen Campbell and Tammy Wynette, and who slept with each other without regard to the usual fidelities, were often beaten up by people dressed as cowboys. Several of my high-school friends, camping on Corral Creek east of Sun Valley that summer, had been hospitalized after being mistaken for hippies by a group of men in cowboy clothes wielding baseball bats.

But the main reason I didn't want to be mistaken for a hippie was that I didn't feel like one. What I saw in the mirror of the women's restroom told me that my identity lay in a place that was deeper and darker. Once, having restocked the toilet paper and finished scrubbing the toilets, the sinks, and the floor, I paused to wash my hands, slick back my hair, and comb my goatee to a point. I went to the mirror, looked out from under the brim of my cowboy hat, and smiled an evil smile.

The thing that lived there smiled an evil smile back. I smiled again. Its smile grew broader.

It was real. And it had achieved an existence independent from me, and in some ways a better existence. It didn't have to pay rent or pump gas or scrub toilets for a living. It lived quite happily in the mirror, having learned some great trick of self-sustenance.

I am at a time in my life when people confess things to me. I have listened to stories of sugar poured into gas tanks, windows broken, siblings disowned, sex out of marriages and within families, pets poisoned, hippies beaten up with baseball bats, photo albums burned, and parents dishonored.

And the motive for those confessions is that evil sometimes comes into our lives only half-invited. We feel as though we have to take all responsibility for it, not to own up to our sin, but to gain some sense of control over evil, to be prepared if evil ever comes in that form again. And while I know there are people in the world who have gotten comfortable with evil, most of us have to settle for becoming comfortable with confession.

Near the end of that long-ago summer, I began to have occasional blinding rages. On the surface, the reason for them was that I needed more sleep. My cabin in Stanley was close enough to the bars that people would park their cars in front of it. After the bars closed, those people would sit on my doorstep and talk all night.

For a week or two I got up out of bed and asked them politely to leave. But one Saturday night I got up and asked the four people sitting outside my door to get off my step and go home so I could get some sleep before work in the morning. They laughed, called me a hippie, and said they'd go home when they felt like it. They didn't feel like it just then.

I went back inside, grabbed a pistol from a kitchen cabinet, jacked a shell into the barrel, took it out on the step, and pressed it against the nearest forehead.

"Go away or I'll kill you," I said. But I didn't recognize my own voice. Somebody else was speaking.

My life would have gone much differently if they had done anything other than leave. But they left, backing slowly toward their car, looking at me with eyes that no longer saw a funny adolescent dressed in funny clothes, with wisps of hair flying about his mouth and nose. They drove away, drunk enough not to go directly to the Custer County sheriff. I did wake up one morning a week later to find a bullet hole through the front wall of my cabin, through an Indian-print blanket I was using as a room divider, and through the back wall.

It was toward the very end of the summer that the two waitresses who lived in a trailer across the alley from my cabin got a dog, a young Samoyed, that barked when chained up and left alone. One night, neither of the waitresses came home. The dog barked constantly, keeping me awake, and at four in the morning I decided to kill it.

I tiptoed out into the alley with the pistol but heard laughter and music from the Stanley Club. It wasn't uncommon in those days for that establishment to stay open well after closing time. The bar would close once and the blinds would come down. People would walk around to the back door, the bar would open, and the party would begin again. Without any reason to think so, I decided the dog's owners were in the Stanley Club, laughing and drinking while their dog barked and I tried to sleep.

When I appeared in the back door, I was waving the gun back and forth and pointing it at the ceiling. I had pulled on my cowboy boots and my leather pants and sheepskin vest. The pewter peace sign was clinking against the Christopher medal on my bare chest. I had on my hat and my sunglasses, even though they were making it hard to see in the dim light.

"Which one of you owns that dog?" I said.

Nobody said a word.

"It's been barking all night," I said. "I'm going to kill it."

One of the cocktail waitresses, an older woman named B.J.—all I remember are the initials she went by—said, "Don't kill that dog." She said it in a voice weary with sadness, as if she had seen many dogs killed in her lifetime. She had smiled and said hello to me when I had eaten in the café or had seen her around town.

Then the pistol went off, putting a small hole in the roof of the Stanley Club bar.

"Call the sheriff," somebody said.

"We can't call the sheriff," said the owner of the club. "I'll lose my license." Then, in an act of complete self-assurance, he grabbed a sawn-off pool cue from under the bar and came around the bar toward me.

I ran. I ran out the door and across a back lot and down the alley, where the dog was still barking. When I got near it, it stopped barking and ran toward me, tail wagging, until it hit the end of its chain. It sat down and waited for me. I grabbed the chain and unhooked it. The dog ran off.

The consequences attending to this incident were mild compared to what they could have been. The owner of the Stanley Club called me a hippie and told me to never come into his café again. B.J., the cocktail waitress, quit being friendly to me when she saw me in the post office. People in town who talked about hippies, who had seldom talked to me, stopped talking to me at all. The sheriff's deputy assigned to Stanley would show up at the Texaco station and drive slowly between the pumps and the building where I sat, setting off the customer alarm but never stopping. He'd be back on the highway by the time I got out the door. The dog across the alley was given away.

The biggest consequence of that night was that I began to

feel ashamed of myself. I began to think of how close I had come to killing the dog. I began to cringe when I thought about it, because it would have been a mindless and heartless little twitch that would have sealed the matter of who I was once and for all. In the mirror, I began to see what B.J. had seen when she looked at me that night.

At the age I am now, I know that we are born into lives that are strongly bound by fate. Free will, if it exists, is a matter of enormous effort or great quantities of dumb luck. When I was sixteen, I was acting on what I thought was my own free will, but it was almost pure fate. And if I have free will at the moment, it's because of dumb luck.

By September, the cars coming into the Texaco station had dwindled to one or two every hour. My hair had hit my shoulders. But my boss had given up on me as a source for drugs. He wasn't calling me a hippie any longer. The two of us would sit in the station drinking the beer he stored in the pop machine. On one warm, quiet, sunny afternoon, he mentioned that he had a twenty-five-pound keg of black powder stored in the attic of the station.

With little else to do, we began by making a cannon out of an eight-foot length of seamless steel tubing. We welded one end of it shut. We would pour an ounce of black powder down the barrel, tamp a paper towel down on top of the powder for wadding, and then put in old flashlight batteries, nuts and bolts, or pieces of rebar. We would then prop it in a squirrel hole fifty yards from the station, lean it in the general direction of the Stanley cemetery, and touch it off with dynamite fuse. The cannon would produce a heavy thud, whatever we had put in the barrel would disappear forever, and the paper towel would come flaming down from the sky, setting the sagebrush on fire where it landed.

Within a week, we had overloaded the cannon with too much gunpowder and too many railroad spikes. With a great roar, the cannon had blown the plug out of its breech, and the length of tubing had shot a hundred yards through the air end over end and stuck itself upright in the middle of Valley Creek. That was when we decided to build a rocket.

In the attic of my cabin I found an old empty fire extinguisher, which had once contained high-pressure carbon dioxide. It was a long narrow white cylinder with a fiberboard cone at one end, and it looked a lot like a rocket.

We managed to get three pounds of black powder into the fire extinguisher. I had been afraid that the nozzle at the end would be too small for the rocket to function well, so we had drilled it out to three-eighths of an inch. We took our rocket out to the same squirrel hole the cannon had blown up in, stuck a length of fuse in the nozzle, lit it, and retired to the Texaco station.

We could see the tip of the rocket above the sagebrush, and it seemed to jerk a little about the time we figured burning fuse would hit gunpowder. But then there was a bright orange ball of flame, eight feet in diameter, where the sagebrush had been. The shock wave that hit us a microsecond later was a bone-shaking slap followed by the screaming roar of a giant explosion. Sounds of splintering wood came from the roof. The passenger-side window of a wrecked car parked beside the station turned into glittering crystals and fell out of its frame. About the time I realized that our rocket had blown up I became aware of the high, loud whine of shrapnel moving at high speed in the direction of Stanley.

My boss and I looked at each other. Things had not gone as planned.

"You better go up and see if we killed anybody," he said.

A number of people were standing on the second-story balcony of the Mountain Village Motel. I drove up, got out of the Mustang, and asked them what had happened.

"Did you see that lightning strike down there?" A man pointed toward the Texaco station. A number of small, benign, puffy clouds were hovering over Sawtooth Valley that day. I was glad to see them.

"We thought it was up here," I said.

At ground zero there was a bushel-sized hole in the ground, with radiating trails razor-cut through the grass and sagebrush by pieces of high-speed metal. We found holes in the station, one of them dead center in the door to the women's restroom. I opened the door and looked in. A square of torn steel was stuck in the far wall. Thousands of shards of mirror glinted up from the floor.

We heard later that a cow had been found dead in a field up above town. But cows were often found dead up there, and this one had been found dead after a hot week, and no one had wanted to get close enough to do an autopsy. The rancher blamed it on hippies.

Toward the end of September, at the last possible moment, I decided to go to college. I hadn't planned on going to college, but it had suddenly come up as an escape from what I had been that summer.

It came as a surprise to me that I wanted to escape the person in the mirror. In June, I had found joy in becoming someone different, in creating a person that was both me and not-me at the same time. By September, that joy had begun to be mixed with fear.

Now, of course, I can see that what I went through that summer was not unique. People do create the people that consume their lives. It's just that the person I had created, leering there in the full-length mirror of the women's room, was so bad, so pathetically patched together, so laughably tacky, such a jumble of counterculture castoffs and dangerous ideas culled from John Wayne movies that somehow I was able to escape being devoured by him.

There are times, when I'm not shuddering at what that person did, that I shudder at what I might have become if my first year away from home had seen me construct a successful nice guy, who followed all the rules, got a neat haircut, shaved, dressed in blue jeans and a cowboy shirt, who only committed violence against hippies and who smiled at the customers and made them feel welcome. That person would have been much more difficult to escape, and when I think of all the other adolescents who have constructed people of their own, so much better than the one I made, I don't think that there are many people in the world who escape their own creations.

I do have some understanding of the people who make

bombs, not because there is any connection between shattering mirrors and escaping one's fate, but because it is so tempting to think that there is. That moment of destruction, when the bomb goes off and the mirror becomes shards and somehow we are still intact, alive, and part of the future— that's a moment of pure being, a moment when the self glows with its own light, when it isn't reflecting anything.

Whitewater
by Horse

THE CHAIN HACKAMORE is a cruel piece of machinery, consisting of a leather harness that goes around the head, short chains that attach to the harness, and a steel ring that the chains slide through. Resistance to being led causes the chains to bite deep into the nose and lip. The pain increases with the degree of resistance.

A chain hackamore breaks an animal to lead quickly, and when you've got a lot of animals in one string, having chain hackamores on everybody keeps everybody moving. Nobody can decide to sit down and bring the whole operation to a stop.

But the summer I was eighteen I used a chain hackamore for a far harsher purpose. I tied Festus, the giant mule entrusted to me by the U.S. Forest Service, to a tree and began beating him with a length of two-by-four. He'd back away, the rope would wind around the tree, the hackamore would tighten, and I'd hit him again. Within a few seconds, his head was flattened against the tree trunk, chains were winding into his lower lip, drawing blood, and his breath was coming in hoarse screams. I bounced the two-by-four off his head and neck and shoulders and ribs until I couldn't lift it anymore.

When I was done, the only thing that kept Festus upright was the rope.

You might think that I felt shame at that moment, but I didn't. I thought I'd just killed Festus, and I was glad. Unfortunately, Festus was government property, a young, healthy, just-purchased mule, one of the biggest any of us at the ranger station had ever seen, able to pack an entire elk if he ever got packed down enough that he could be handled. I would be fired from my job as a Forest Service packer unless I could come up with an excuse for a dead mule covered with two-by-four marks. My career as a government employee would end when I showed up at the Seafoam guard station with one less mule than I had started with. I was also missing George, my saddle horse.

I should state right here that I know that it's not right to torture animals in chain hackamores. I have a minister friend, Enright, who went so far as to shoot a man who shot Henry, his horse. Enright was walking up to Henry, about to put his foot in the stirrup, when Henry fell over. When the hunter who had killed Henry came running up the hill, he found Enright with one foot on Henry's carcass.

"That's my elk," said the hunter. "Get your foot off it." Enright pointed to Henry's saddle. The guy started running back down the hill, and Enright unholstered his .22 pistol and shot him in the ass.

Enright only had to do a little county jail time for this incident, because he drove his flesh-wounded victim to the emergency clinic in Stanley, lecturing him all the way about the evil that attends killing an innocent beast of burden. At the civil trial, Enright's attorney noted Enright's status as an emissary of God, quoted Walt Whitman and the Bible, and spoke at length on the suffering of dumb and loyal animals. The jury awarded the victim a dollar.

After Enright got out of jail he had a period of unemployment. He spent it hunting chukar partridges. After hunting chukars in the hills around the East Fork of the Salmon, chasing them up steep slopes only to have them vanish into rockpiles and sagebrush, after missing them on the wing and then missing them on the ground, he told me that chukars were creatures of Satan.

"The only way to hunt them is in the egg," he said. Even Enright's concern for the weak and helpless had its flaws.

But not for nothing do we learn that most serial killers have a history of torturing frogs and kittens when they were children. Not for nothing do we turn from the presence of men who break the noses and black the eyes of their wives and from the presence of the wives who stay with them. Not for nothing do we avert decent faces away from those who dance the weeping, bloody, ancient dance of the powerful and the powerless, and I remember that summer I was eighteen with a shudder, because nothing I will ever do will stop it from being the summer I tied an animal in a chain hackamore to a tree and beat him with a club.

Nothing will change the fact that Festus was a bad mule, either. When we first put a packsaddle on him in the Forest Service corrals, he broke a halter rope and bucked the saddle off inside of a minute. When we tied him back up and cinched the saddle on him as tight as we could, we were only able to pack him by throwing him down on one side, tying his kicking feet to the fence, and lashing a canvas-wrapped bale of hay to the top side of the saddle. Then we had to throw him down on the other side, lash another bale to the saddle, and finally let him up. Then we put a chain hackamore on him and trailed him ten miles behind a pickup, until he was dragging, bleeding from unshod feet, covered with foamy sweat and broken blisters, and the desperate wheeze of his breath could be heard in the pickup cab.

The irony of breaking a mule this way lay in the fact that I thought I was a good man with horses. I had watched my father break horses gently, working them with light hands, talking them into accepting the saddle and his presence on their backs. When it came time to put a packsaddle on them, he had usually touched and fed them and ridden them enough so that they were curious rather than outraged when the straps were slipped down around their rumps and across their chests. I thought I could talk to horses that way. I thought they would understand me in the same way—that my father's ability to break horses was hereditary.

But I was working with two Forest Service foremen who prided themselves on being real cowboys, and even though I had been hired because I knew how to pack horses, it was clear that they didn't think much of my skills with mules.

They knew how to break mules, they told me. They showed me their methods and at the end of a few weeks I was just as brutal to the animals as they were.

When they put me out on the Middle Fork of the Salmon with a string of fourteen mules, Festus was among them. I was also trailing two Percheron colts that were too young to work. People who worked in the Forest Supervisors' offices in Challis and Boise would use the mules to pack in elk and deer that fall, and they wanted them packed down by the time hunting season rolled around. They wanted the Percherons gentle enough to pull the horse-drawn equipment in the Forest Service pastures on the abandoned ranches on the Middle Fork.

My job was to supply trail crews in what is now the Frank Church Wilderness, mostly along the Middle Fork, from Dagger Falls to the mouth of Loon Creek. I packed chain saws, trail graders, tents, food, harnesses, bedrolls, culverts, treated timber, and a complete kitchen and table service for eight, in green-and-white Forest Service glass, on those mules. On the evenings that I wasn't near a corral, I would hobble the mules and run them up a tributary canyon, pitching my tent at its mouth. I would put bells on the lead mules, and I got so that I would come instantly out of a deep sleep if I heard a bell come too close. But there had been times I had slept while they had filed down past my tent and onto the trail. Once, by the time I had caught up with them, they had gone fifteen miles in hobbles, back to Thomas Creek, the last place they'd had good pasture. I learned then that a mule can go faster in hobbles than a man can go in cowboy boots.

The saddle horse they gave me was twenty-five years old. His name was George, and he was a slow, gentle old sway-backed sorrel gelding with arthritis in his shoulders. Riding him downhill started him into a side-to-side dance that produced little forward movement, and I soon learned to dismount at the slightest decline.

But other than that, George was all the horse I wanted. Down below Thomas Creek, the rattlesnakes were thick and the slope was so steep on the high side of the trail that I could hear them—but not see them—buzzing in the rocks a foot or two from my thigh. George would hear them, step away, and keep us both from harm, never breaking stride.

In the mornings, when I filled the grain bucket, George would be waiting outside my tent. His teeth were getting short and he was losing weight. I'd give him more than his share of grain, put a halter on him, swing up on his bare back, and go get the mules.

Atop George, I was able to see a world marked by brittle sage and broken rock, by high summits still covered with June snow, by dry thunderclouds and the high dark crescent shapes of hawks. And that was just on the rattlesnake side of the trail. On the river side, there was the flash of falling water, the white sand of riverside beaches, and the occasional drifting boats of the Middle Fork rafters.

It occurred to me, when I saw them, that the rafters were better off than me. After all, I had to work all day with half-wild mules and all they had to do was drink beer and watch the world float by.

There were times when I rode along stretches of rapids so rough that boats had been known to turn somersaults down them. Then—even if I was working the mules around a sharp cliffside corner a hundred feet above the water—I tended toward smug self-congratulation. A careful old horse can inspire smugness, even love, when your ears are ringing with the roar of whirlpools and the screams of people suddenly convinced they should have vacationed at a shuffleboard park.

I began to think that George and I could read each other's thoughts. I also began to think that he was getting thinner and thinner and that before the summer was over, if I kept riding him ten or fifteen miles a day, he'd be ready for the knacker.

By July, no lives had been lost in the waterfalls of the Middle Fork. And nights, when I had hobbled the mules and had eaten my dinner of canned Spam and macaroni and cheese, I walked to where I could see campfires down on the sandbars. I heard guitars and laughter, and smelled sirloin.

I was a happiness voyeur. More than that I was a person astonished that two worlds could touch and yet remain separate. Twenty feet from where salmon sped upstream under the drifting boats, riverbank ferns gave way to grass and the occasional grazing deer, and twenty feet from there grew the stunted thick leaves of desert plants. Out on the water the sun warmed, but on the trail it dried and it burned.

A week before the day I tied Festus to the tree I had put the mules up a tributary canyon. In the morning when I went out to catch them, George wasn't waiting outside my tent. After I had the mules tied up, I tracked George's big hoofprints on up the canyon until, a couple of hours later, I reached the summit. George was there, and he looked up

at me from the tiny meadow of short dry grass he was standing in.

"George," I said, and waved his halter at him. He stood
still. I didn't have grain with me, but he'd never been hard to
catch before. He looked at me sadly and turned his skinny
rump to me and walked away, into the next drainage.

"George!" I yelled. But he was beyond hearing me. I
could have caught him. Even in cowboy boots I could outrun
him. But I was thinking he was going off to die. I thought
there would be some good in letting him go. I thought
maybe I could get one of the Percherons to let me put a saddle on him.

I walked back down to camp and began packing up. The
experiment with the Percheron lasted somewhat less than
eight seconds and would have been entertainment if anybody other than the mules had been there to see it. I ended
up riding a short mule named Johnny, and the dust beneath
his hooves was deep and fine that week. Johnny didn't avoid
the rattlesnakes, which now buzzed within striking distance
of my neck. I didn't think that I would miss George, but I
did.

In the evenings, after I had unpacked, I began to search for
George in the high desert mountains above the river. There,
I found old mines, a ruined fire lookout, small hillside springs
that nourished, with tiny amounts of water, the wild orchards
of abandoned homesteads. I found a rotting trapper's cabin
at the intersection of two overgrown trails, with rusty traps
still hanging on an inside wall. I found trees that had grown
around horseshoes hung on their branches, caves littered
with deer bones, and ancient ridge-top forests, twisted, small,
and wind whipped. The sunsets that summer were fiery, and

the water, looking like molten lead in the bottom of the canyon, reflected red light onto dusk-gray hillsides. When I had finished hunting for George for an evening, I would walk down into darkness, put the bells on the lead mules, and go to bed.

The day I tied Festus to the tree had begun at daylight, and it had taken me until two in the afternoon to get the mules saddled and packed. I was heading from Indian Creek to Thomas Creek, a distance which would allow me to trail down the river, unpack, and settle in by dark.

But I made a mistake. I usually packed the trail grader, plow, single-tree, and chains on Festus, which all together weighed a couple of hundred pounds and couldn't be damaged by anything short of a cutting torch. But that day I packed the kitchen on him. I suppose I did it to be able to brag about it later—I was going to tell my two foremen that I had packed the kitchen boxes on the same mule we'd had to throw down to pack.

Festus had been a decent mule for a while. He was so tall I had had to pack him standing on a rock or a stump, but other than that he had been little trouble. He led well—the chain hackamore had done its work on his lower lip—and he hadn't bucked anything off for a week.

But just as I was tying him into the string, Festus began bucking. He broke the piggin string that attached him to the next mule. He bucked his way out into a clearing, and then he began bucking in earnest. The plates and cups and bottles inside the kitchen boxes started clanging and tinkling, and first one box and then the other arced out and away from his saddle and crashed into the ground. Then Festus got the saddle twisted down under him and went into a frenzy of kicking, twisting, and crow-hopping, breaking straps and dragging the saddle through the rocks until finally the last pieces of it fell off him.

I walked toward him slowly. In the softest of voices, I told him it was all right. Putting the kitchen on him was my mistake. As soon as I picked everything up, I'd pack him up again with the grader and plow, and we'd get on the trail. He let me put a rope through the ring in his hackamore, and I led him to a tree and tied him to it.

But as I left him and walked back to the pieces of saddle that littered the clearing, he kicked me. His hoof caught me hard in my upper thigh.

I came off the ground long enough to realize I was flying. Then I hit and rolled. I lay there, thinking that my femur was broken and that I was going to die—a broken femur will lose enough blood into the thigh muscle that you can bleed to death without even a break in the skin—and I was alone. Pretty soon the flies would be feasting on me, and the only time I'd ever float the Middle Fork would be when they floated my body out, and I wouldn't get to enjoy it because I would be dead. Festus had remembered the day that he'd first been made into a pack animal and had bided his time, and now had had his revenge.

I wasn't nearly as patient as he had been. I crawled over to a camp table and pulled a two-by-four brace out from under it. I used it as a crutch to get to my feet, and limped and hobbled toward Festus.

By the time I was done my leg still hurt but I was feeling a lot better. I took the rope off Festus's hackamore and untied it from the tree. He fell over on his side and lay there unmoving.

I packed the kitchen on another mule, put a canvas around Festus's torn-up saddle, packed it on top of the kitchen, and finished tying the string together. When I was done I saddled Johnny and away we went. Five miles later I decided that I should have towed Festus to the Middle Fork and claimed that he fell in and drowned. But then I decided that I had had enough of mules, enough of being the only human being in camp, enough of the Middle Fork, and enough of the Forest Service. If they wouldn't fire me, I'd quit.

At Thomas Creek the next morning, I got out of my tent, stood up, and found myself face-to-face with Festus. He had followed us downriver—at a distance—and he looked terrible. I put George's halter on him and put him at the end of the string, without a packsaddle, and led him for a couple of days. Then, only partly because I was getting tired of the dust that rose up around Johnny's shoulders and swirled into my face, I put my riding saddle on Festus, put my foot in the stirrup, and swung up on top of him. I expected to die then and there.

A mule always rides more smoothly than a horse, and Festus was smooth riding for a mule. He was surefooted and though he didn't avoid the rattlesnakes, he was enough taller than Johnny that they would have had to stretch to get to me. For a week I waited for him to turn on me and buck me into a nest of snakes or wait until I wasn't watching and then kick me to the top of the nearest Ponderosa. But he never did. He understood the reins and he wasn't in the least bit hardmouthed. I began to think Festus and I could read each other's thoughts.

It was still July when I reached Rapid River, one of the main tributaries of the Upper Middle Fork, and camped with the trail crew that was working there. There, in the middle of the week, the news came over the Forest Service radio that we had an unexpected day off. I left my animals with the trail crew. They promised not to lose any of them. They also told me if George showed up they'd put him in the corral.

On foot, I climbed up out of Rapid River, climbed against the clock, climbed 4,000 vertical feet, and climbed finally up the steps of the farthest-from-civilization fire lookout of them all, Little Soldier. Its lonely occupant welcomed me in, shook my hand, and made me tea. Then, while he scanned a ragged horizon for signs of burning forest and I scanned it for signs of George, he turned on his battery-powered radio and we listened in awe on the day men first talked from the moon.

It was winter before George turned up in Challis. The Forest Service put him out to pasture, and he lived another half-decade, giving rides to Forest Service children and eating rolled oats. The cowboys congratulated me for what I had done with Festus—he packed out two elk that hunting season. But I stayed away from him. I thought for a long time that he was just waiting for the right moment and that then he was going to kill a human being, any human being, but preferably me. The next summer I got a different job, as a wilderness ranger in the Sawtooths. I was on foot, carrying a backpack, and in the nearly thirty years between the time I took the club to Festus and now, I can count on my fingers the times I've been in a saddle. I've never lost my temper with an animal since that day.

Since that summer, I've read Walt Whitman and I have come to love the 32nd poem in his *Song of Myself* that says he could turn and live with the animals, because

They do not sweat and whine about their condition,
They do not lie awake in the dark and weep for their sins,
They do not make me sick discussing their duty to God,
Not one is dissatisfied, not one is demented with the mania
*   of owning things,*
Not one kneels to another, nor to his kind that lived thousands
*   of years ago,*
Not one is respectable or unhappy over the whole earth.

Without ever knowing the story of my encounter with Festus, my minister friend Enright has told me that he has come to believe that animals are morally superior to human beings, especially human beings like him and me. And although Enright dearly loves to hunt, he has finally given up hunting.

"Life is a spiritual journey," he tells me. "Live long enough and you'll give up killing your fellow creatures."

"What about chukars?"

"The chukar partridge is a creature of God," he says, "when you're not chukar hunting."

It's no use talking to him about it. He has sold his guns—one of them, the .22 pistol, he sold to me.

"Don't shoot anybody with it," he said, handing it to me. "Unless they shoot your horse."

Lately, Enright has become enamored of the story of Jonah. He preaches on it all the time, and his congregation has become sick of hearing how Jonah, disobeying God's call, got on a boat to someplace else, became the worst kind of bad luck for the boat he was on, got thrown overboard, got eaten by a whale, and was regurgitated, not much worse for wear, at the place he had been told to go in the first place.

"The story of Jonah," Enright says, "proves that God has us all in a chain hackamore."

I tell him the story of Jonah was a good enough metaphor in the first place and he doesn't need to mix it with another. But he does have a point. If life really is a spiritual journey, it's probably a lot like Jonah's cruise. Things happen to us even after we've refused them. Deep internal imperatives take us in directions we would never consciously choose, and maybe those deep internal imperatives are another way of saying God. Enright, who loves to hunt, now finds himself unable to reconcile himself to the killing of animals. Who or what told him to become the nonhunter he has become? Who told him to turn and live with the animals?

And yet I have learned that it isn't that easy. You can't just turn and live with the animals because you want to. Their world and ours, though close, do not often touch, and it's seldom that they are bridged by anything other than violence. I would never tell Enright that to really know a chukar you have to shoot and eat it and that to really share thoughts with a mule you have to beat him with a two-by-four, but at some level my experience has taught me these things, and at some level I resist taking the next step on my spiritual journey because at some level I'm not sure who it is who has me by the nose.

Sawtooth Stories

DRIVE TWO MILES WEST out of Stanley on Highway 21 and go left at the Iron Creek turnoff. Drive up to the Iron Creek trailhead. Follow that trail almost a mile to the sign at the edge of the Sawtooth Wilderness. Then look to your left and you'll see where I lived one summer thirty years ago.

It's just a small flat spot on the bank of Iron Creek now. It's crisscrossed by fallen logs. The wooden tent frame that was once there has been torn down. Its boards have been packed out to the trailhead and trucked away. No artifact remains. No one sleeps there at the edge of the wild anymore.

But if you can, think of it as it was in 1970: There is a tent frame at the spot, with a white canvas wall tent stretched over it, and smoke rises from a stovepipe sticking out of the roof. Inside, a fire burns in a sheepherder's stove. Beside the stove is an army-surplus cot, and on the cot is a sleeping bag.

A bag of books—good books, the hard core of a summer reading list sent to me by the English Department of Harvard University—spills open under the cot. Harvard is the institution I've transferred to for the sole reason of getting out of Idaho without getting into Vietnam.

The kitchen stretches along one tent wall. It's a long table laden with Campbell's soup cans, pots and dishpans, Bisquick, silverware, spaghetti sauce, lemonade packets, detergent, and cases and cases of Fig Newtons. There is a rocking chair. The late light of a June sunset still glows through the canvas.

I am in the tent, sitting in the chair, reading from *The Myth of Sisyphus*, by Albert Camus. He's on the list, right after Beckett and Buber, and I'm having a better time with him than I had with the first two. Camus's title essay recounts the myth of a man who cheats death. Sisyphus, its hero, goes AWOL from Hades and lives on the bright surface of the earth, enjoying each stolen day as it comes, feeling the sun warm on his back and the clear air entering his lungs, delighting in the light and clouds and water as he sits on a promontory over the ocean, waiting for the gods to catch up with him. Of course, they eventually do.

And when they do, they devise the most cruel punishment they can think of. They take him back to dark Hades and condemn him to roll a huge boulder to the narrow top of its tallest mountain. When he gets the boulder up there, it tips away from him and rolls back to the bottom. He has to walk down and roll it back up. Forever. That's his job. That's his life.

As I sit there, rocking and reading, I am enjoying this

book, because I'm a Forest Service wilderness ranger and I'm hiking five miles back up to Sawtooth Lake in the morning. I have already been there today, and yesterday, and the day before yesterday. It's my job to stay in that tent and hike up to Sawtooth Lake every day, talking to every tourist I encounter on the trail. I have a set speech, the substance of which is: "Welcome to the Sawtooths. Please pack out what you pack in. Don't yell and scream all night. Don't get naked in front of the children of strangers. Don't try to burn used disposable diapers in your campfires because they will not burn no matter how much you would like them to. Don't cut down any trees. Don't tie your horse in the middle of someone else's campsite. Stay on the trails. Don't cut the switchbacks. Don't fall off a cliff and please enjoy yourself."

Every day, on my way to Sawtooth Lake, I give versions of this speech eighty or ninety or a hundred times. Every day, on my way back to my tent on Iron Creek, I pull half-burned plastic diapers out of still-smoking campfires and pick up beer cans, plastic ponchos, insecticide foggers, spent cartridges, and aluminum foil. Behind my tent is a great and growing mound of garbage, which I will pack down to the transfer camp when the season ends in September. I will have this job again next summer.

Sisyphus and I, I'm thinking, are brothers.

Camus ends the essay by saying that Sisyphus transcends his struggle with the gods. If he's got an eternity of rolling the boulder up the mountain, he's got an eternity to make that boulder *his* boulder, that mountain *his* mountain, and his life during those walks back down an endless sequence of freedoms.

But it's 1970. I'm not yet twenty years old. I don't understand the nature of time and inevitability. What I am really focused on is the first part of the essay, where Sisyphus escapes death and goes to sit on the edge of the sun-glittering sea for as long as he can get away with it.

I am planning my own escape. I'm going to go East to college. I'm going to become a professor. I'm going to write books, read books, collect books. I'll live in the light of my own education and flee from the routine of packing garbage out of the Sawtooths. And I'll have the summers off.

It's 1970. A war is raging, and each day pushes its burden of hope before it.

That summer is distant now on the scale of human lifetimes. In the interim I've realized that the really good part of Camus's essay is the part where Sisyphus learns to love his punishment. I'm amazed at how easily the gods find you when they want you, how your own time AWOL seems to have been an integral part of their plan, and how quickly they put you to work at an inescapable task. I'm a professor of English now, and I teach writing in college now, and if ever there was the perfect analogue to Sisyphus starting back up the mountain with his boulder, it's that moment when I pick up that first page of the first freshman essay, on the first Friday of fall term. *What I did on my summer vacation. . . .*

What I did on my summer vacation in 1970 was hike up to Sawtooth Lake forty or fifty times. I packed out a half-ton of garbage. I issued tickets to two people who had ridden motorcycles to the creek crossing below Alpine Lake. I cleaned up campsites and identified strangled plants for Boy

Scouts trying to get their Botany merit badges. I found lost children and told people where to find the fish in Sawtooth and Alpine Lakes. I read through the reading list that Harvard had sent me and thought I was wiser for it.

But I read too many of those books the way I had first read Camus—I identified with the characters in those books who tried to cheat fate. There's one of them in every great work of literature, and I saw myself in every one of those characters in turn. I didn't pay much attention to what happened to them toward the end of their stories.

In another essay, Camus focuses on Kirilov, one of Dostoyevsky's heroes, who is so unhappy with the world he lives in that he obliterates it by blowing out his own brains with a pistol. It works for him. Dostoyevsky's joke on Kirilov is that the book keeps going on even after Kirilov doesn't.

I had grown up on a ranch in rural Idaho. My parents had spent their lives working. I was set to do the same. But I had been accepted—anointed, really—by Harvard. If there was ever a way for an Idaho boy to cheat fate, death, time, the gods, obliterate his world, this was it.

Now, of course, I look at that summer in the cozy tent, with its supply of food and firewood, its fifty good books, and its location on the trail to Sawtooth Lake, and it seems to me that it was the one time in my life that I was free and that I willingly walked away from it.

I have an uneasy suspicion about Sisyphus, now. I think that maybe the gods didn't have to go after him. I think maybe he just showed up one day at the gates of Hell, asking for something to do.

. . .

But in August of that summer, I really did conceive something that even now seems like an escape. I had discovered that I could drop over the crumbling ridge that separates Iron Creek from Crooked Creek and find myself at a small shallow lake where no tourists ever went. Each morning, I would contact 100 of the hikers that by then looked to me like lemmings headed for a mass drowning in Sawtooth Lake. I would give them my spiel, wave the last of the 100 good-bye, climb up the sandy couloir that led to the lowest saddle between the two drainages, drop down the other side, and spend the afternoon reading and sunning myself on the decomposed granite boulder that rose from the center of the lake.

During those August afternoons, I was free of responsibility, free of clothes, free of any twinges of conscience about not working because I had filled my quota of public contacts for the day. I would lie on the boulder in bright sunlight until I got too warm. Then I would wade to the bank, holding my book above my head, and lie on the rough warm sand until the shadows of the high cliffs above the lake touched the water. I was only a few hundred yards away from the Iron Creek trail, but it was a few hundred yards of solid granite, and I never encountered anyone else there at that small lake in Crooked Creek.

I have tried to remember what I thought about during those afternoons of reading on the rock, and I can't recall that I thought about anything. The words that I read went through my head and became the world. The other world, the one where I stretched out naked on a rock, that world of wind-curled trees, sand, water, and sky, held no words.

I spent hours in the rich, intriguing, separate realities of books. I didn't think about the passage of time or of the moment of exploding possibility when I would get on a plane in Boise and get off in Boston. I didn't think about the garbage I had cached below the Iron Creek trail that I would have to pack out to the tent that evening. I owned those books like Camus says Sisyphus owns his rock.

Do not think that I was having anything remotely resembling a wilderness experience. A wilderness experience was one of the options listed on our Forest Service sign-in sheets at the registration box at the trailhead. If you visited the Sawtooths, you were asked why you were there. You could check the box marked hunting, or fishing, or hiking, or photography, or horseback riding. If you checked none of these, you were, by default, seeking a wilderness experience.

What a wilderness experience was depended on who was seeking it. It could have all the complexity of a novel. A few wilderness experiencers packed guns—big ones, 7 mm magnums or .357s, strapped to the outside of their packs. They weren't hunters. It was the wrong season for big game. When I met them, our dialogue would go like this:

"How come the gun?"

"Bears."

I would shake my head. "No bears up there."

This was never taken as good news.

"There might be bears up there," they would say.

"No bears," I would say.

"Cougars?" they would ask, hopefully.

"No cougars," I would say.

"There might be cougars," they would say.

"Please don't shoot around the lakes," I would say. "It makes the other campers nervous."

That night I would hear the faint rolling echoes of gunshots come down the canyon from the lakes. There were things out there in the dark that only some people could see.

At the campsites, after dinner had been cooked and the tents had been set up, people would begin to build things. At that time, wood fires were allowed at Sawtooth and Alpine Lakes, and usually what they built were giant rock fireplaces, with chimneys and carefully calibrated cooking surfaces. They would pile up great stacks of firewood and then begin to line the trails with leftover rocks. They would carve their names in trees, dam the creeks, build bridges where no bridges had been before, or go up the mountainsides above the lakes and trundle rocks down into the water right next to people who were flyfishing. They would build teepee frames when they didn't have teepees, and tables when they didn't have anything to put on them. After a while I figured out that this frenzy of activity took place about the time that most of these people would be sitting down to watch TV if they were home.

They didn't spend the time talking with each other or watching the sunset or listening to the waves lap against the driftwood that jammed the outlets of the lakes. But they had a wilderness experience.

I finally decided having a wilderness experience meant

imposing one's self upon the wild, and if it meant moving a ton of rock or killing an animal, so be it.

There were others, hiking through from Grandjean or Atlanta, who told me how far they had gone, how many days they had been out, and how far they were going. Climbers who had just finished with Mount Regan, which rears up over the south end of Sawtooth Lake, pointed at it, shrugged it off, and told me which peak they would bag next. Almost everything anybody did or said out there was part of civilization.

Everyone is living out his or her own story on the trail. Stories are artifice, and when you live your own story what you're doing is placing one artifact—the self—within another artifact—the story. You're making a thing like an Oriental carving, a thing like a jade bird with delicate jade feathers enclosed in a cage of woven jade reeds. It's fragile. The whole thing can shatter if you drop it.

Get out in the wild, away from houses, cars, diplomas, software, and jobs. Then stop speaking, lose language, fail to grasp the word, and your self just might begin to slip from your story. We all instinctively know that. It's why people on the Iron Creek Trail tell people they've just met intimate details of their own lives. It's why they carve their names on trees on the shores of Sawtooth Lake. It's why they shoot guns and spray-paint rocks and toss beer cans into twenty feet of crystal-clear water. They're making their stories strong enough to last for a few days in that world.

On the trail in the mornings, I greeted people. I told

them to take care of the Sawtooths. We said good-bye. The sounds we uttered were dead ritual in a dead language. They went to derive meaning from that first bite of steel into living bark. I hastened over the ridge to what was vital and alive for me—my books.

Then it was Labor Day. There was frost on the ground in the mornings. My job ended. I no longer had to climb to Sawtooth Lake and back every day. I no longer carried litter back down the trail. Tourists no longer trudged up from the transfer camp. Their wilderness experiences would have to wait for another summer.

I left my spot beside Iron Creek and went back to my cabin in Stanley. The evening before I was to leave for Boise to get on the plane to Boston, I went down to the Rod and Gun Club, where the bartender knew me. The place was mostly empty, and the bartender and I were shooting pool for beer, staying about even with each other. Near closing time I made a mistake.

"You ever heard of Sisyphus?" I asked. The bartender looked at me like I was a stranger.

"You've changed," he said, "since you've been reading them books."

"It's a Greek story."

"I don't want to talk about *Greek* stories," he said. "I've got a story to tell and it's going to kill me if I don't tell it to somebody."

"Tell it," I said.

"I'm in love," he said. He pointed across the pool table into the Rod and Gun's restaurant. There, sitting at a table, smoking a cigarette, was the waitress, a girl with enormous black hair wearing a black rayon uniform and black fishnet stockings. She hadn't spent the summer out in the middle of a lake getting a tan. But she looked good, sort of. She was the whitest woman I'd ever seen.

"She's seventeen. I'm forty-five. I've got a wife and kids in Boise. I took this job because I thought if I got out of the house and came up here for the summer it might improve my marriage. Now I'm sleeping with a girl who wants me to run back to Reno with her for the winter so she can finish high school."

"Why are you telling me this?" I asked. He didn't hear me.

"So help me God," said the bartender, "I'm going to marry her."

"Go back to your wife and kids," I said. When I said it, it surprised me. It didn't come from anything I had read that summer.

"Life goes by so fast," he said, staring into the restaurant. Then he didn't say anything for a while. Then he said, "You never know when you can just up and die. I could have another heart attack tomorrow."

"Don't do it," I said. I had met his wife once, when she had visited him for a weekend.

The bartender finally looked at me. "Don't worry. I won't. I made it all up. I never even had a heart attack." He stowed his cue in the rack behind the bar.

"I'm done for the evening," he said. "You'd better go home now."

He turned away from me and began washing glasses behind the bar. I walked out of the Rod and Gun and started across the street to my cabin. Halfway there, I turned back.

Through the unshaded window of the restaurant, I watched him walk to her, touch her on the shoulder, and bend to kiss her pale naked neck. That image was more real than anything I'd read all summer. It was the first time I realized that I would ever be any older than the age I was or that I might ever hate being alone. I ran home, staggering as I stepped in potholes in the road and flinching at the noises that came out of the darkness.

Thirty-six hours later, I was on a plane flying out of Boise. I was not in a peaceful frame of mind. That last night in the Rod and Gun had thrown into doubt all the worlds I had lived in when I'd been reading those fifty good books. Still, I was flying East, toward an education and a world and an identity made up entirely of language. It suddenly didn't seem like a good move, and in some ways it never has seemed like a good move. I never have entirely trusted the books I read there, or the lectures I heard there, or the words I wrote there. And although I have come back to Idaho, I still exist in a world constructed of words. It's a world that is more than a little suspect.

Many years after I first read Camus, I finally found his statement that says a man will spend the whole of his life searching for the two or three images that first awakened his soul. I must have seen one of those images that night in Stanley, and although I have no inclination to search for it, it burns in my memory. It reminds me that there is a thing— call it the wild, call it fate, call it the gods or love or the world or the death of all those things—that is far more solid than words. It's far more real than we are.

When Fences Fly

M Y FRIEND ALEX, who grew up on a farm outside of Bliss, Idaho, told me years ago that he would have a million dollars and retire by the time he was thirty. At the time it was a bold prediction. We were both fifteen, and he worked in his family's fields not so he could have a car or go to college, but so there would be food on the family table and diesel in the tractor, and so the farm wouldn't go back to the bank.

Not long after that Alex's father died of lymphoma. The bank took the farm, and Alex had some tough years getting out of high school while playing lineman in eight-man football and working a full-time job. But he managed to get into the College of Idaho, our state's liberal arts college, and through a combination of loans and a football scholarship got his political science degree. On the strength of his undergraduate record he got into Harvard Business School, and by the time he was twenty-six, he was working for an international bank, loaning Saudi oil money to Brazilian cattle ranchers and getting his cut as the money passed through his hands.

On his thirtieth birthday he had in excess of a million dollars. He would have had to sell stocks and property to put it all in one pile, but what the IRS would have taken wouldn't have put him below a million. He was rich beyond my wildest dreams.

I asked him where he planned to retire. I wondered if he was planning to reacquire the old farm and live there in paid-off splendor, skiing at Sun Valley in the winters, fishing on the Salmon River in the summers, and raising cattle, horses, and hay because they looked good in the fields, not because they were required to make interest payments. But he said he wasn't retiring.

"If you've made a million dollars you know how easily and quickly you can lose it," he told me. At the time he had just returned from Moscow, and the poverty of the Russians had shaken him back to his adolescence.

"People there will come up to you on the street and feel the fabric of your suit between their fingers," he said to me. "Not to buy it. Just to *feel* it."

And no, he wasn't going to buy the old farm. "Bliss, Idaho, is just like Saudi Arabia," he said. "Except in Bliss, the wind blows harder and the people aren't any fun."

By the time I was thirty, I had yet to make $20,000 in a single year. Alex told me that the only reason a person of my talents was poor was because I had never felt poor. I told him a person of my talents was poor because I didn't want to be rich.

I quoted Emerson to him. "*Things* are in the saddle," I said, "and ride mankind."

"One of these days you'll start to feel poor," he said. "But then it'll be too late to do anything about it." He smiled. "One of these days you'll wish you hadn't wasted your time teaching."

That was a winter day in a year when interest rates, unemployment, and the price of gold were following an exponential curve. Apocalypse was in the air. I was teaching in a small and exclusive private school in Sun Valley. I was skiing on weekends. I was going with a woman who owned a condo. I was not unhappy.

But after talking to Alex and figuring out what his easily lost million dollars would do at fifteen percent, I began to be obsessed by a small, absurd fantasy that I would wake up one day with the power to pull gold from mountains. I would be able to wave my arm at a mountain and suddenly all the gold it contained would appear refined in the trunk of my car, crushing the rear tires, breaking the rear axle, and levering the front tires off the ground. Not to worry. I would buy a new car. But not before I had sold the gold, paid the taxes on the money, and put what remained in the bank until it accumulated enough interest to buy a new car. And I wouldn't buy the most expensive new car I could find. I would never spend all the interest money I accumulated. I would plow it back into the principal, and I would get richer and richer and richer. And richer. And so on to infinity, or at least until I was 850 years old and owned all the money in the world. On the way there people would whisper about me: "He's worth $12 million. $39 million. $781 million. A billion five."

Even now I marvel at a fantasy that had me breaking the

laws of physics and old age but obeying the regulations of the Internal Revenue Service. But it was a fantasy that gave me a great deal of comfort through some lean years. It was simple, portable, and didn't require a lot of maintenance. Testing it against reality was not a possibility. I was never bothered by all the ghosts of all the people who weren't going to end up with all the money in the world.

I was walking out of the icy school parking lot one day—the lot was on an incline and I was parked a couple of blocks away, on a hill above the highway that ran by the school, because the tires on my old Mustang were bald—when one of my students, a sixteen-year-old girl, drove by me in her new BMW. She had just gotten her driver's license and the car for her birthday. She had the engine redlined. The BMW's studded tires were chewing down through the ice to asphalt, and she was slowly leaving two smoking trenches behind her in the lot. Eventually she burned her way to the highway that ran by the school, caught some traction, and left a cloud of oil smoke all the way to the stoplight on Sun Valley Road. Since that day I've never even been able to *think* about buying a used BMW.

I had been trying in vain to teach her the fundamentals of written English. Someone else must have tried in vain to teach her the fundamentals of driving on ice. She had just ruined a car that had cost more than my annual salary.

At that moment I began to feel poor. I began to feel oddly ashamed of myself for not owning a BMW. I began to feel guilty for being a teacher on a teacher's salary. I began to realize the absurdity of another of my fantasies: that I was making the world a better place by teaching people with much more money than me how to express, in language subtle and beautiful, the self-conscious intricacies of their existence.

I decided that their existences held no intricacy and little self-consciousness. They could afford to push intricacy away, as something that did not quite exist. Only things that could be expressed as profit or loss, as interest paid or interest gained, held substance for them. My student didn't have to know written English because knowing written English would never figure in her survival or her ability to buy a new car or in any description she might need to make of her world. I found myself envying her, with her trust fund and her not-very-good brain and her ability to let the simple arithmetic of finance become her life. And so I kept dreaming of waving the gold out of mountains. But I also, in an instinctive fit of self-preservation, quit my job.

As it happened, I became a bartender at Slavey's Saloon just down the street from the school. It was a good change for me at the time. For one thing, pouring alcohol helped me to a better understanding of rich people. If you put four or five drinks in a person it doesn't matter how much money he or she has—what you have is a drunk, and a rich drunk is about the same as a poor drunk. Their language is that of alcohol, their concerns those of alcohol, and their personalities those of alcohol. I'm not bringing all this up out of self-righteousness, because I drink alcohol too, occasionally in amounts large enough to obliterate my own economic status.

At Slavey's people gave me money, usually about $75 a shift, and with a pocket full of cash I forgot that cash was important. It was simply there when I needed it, and at the end of the season, when I was cleaning out my apartment, I found a couple of uncashed paychecks under my bed. I hadn't put them in an interest-bearing savings account, or in Microsoft stock, or in Krugerrands. I had stopped dreaming that gold would magically appear in the trunk of my car. I had been able to live the closest thing to a money-free existence that our civilization offers, losing myself in the circular, never-ending conversations among friends in bars, eating the free employee meals, drinking the free employee drinks, forgetting the future, forgetting, indeed, that there were any people in the world richer than myself.

So I was able to make a truce with money and the people who had a lot of it, there at Slavey's. I decided that the amount of money anybody needed for a good life was probably a lot less than anybody *thought* they needed. The main thing was not to feel that poverty, that Bliss, Idaho, condition of the soul that had been embedded in my friend Alex when the bank foreclosed and that a million dollars couldn't relieve.

And the other main thing was to get along with other people and treat them well and help them out when you could. You would think that having money would help you to get along with people, treat them well, and help them out, but it doesn't work that way.

One of the things that Alex said about his work as a banker was that the people he met who had made a great deal of money were usually good, usually honest, usually hard-working people. Their children, he said, were less so. And their grandchildren, he said, were monsters. He told me about one woman, the granddaughter of a billionaire, who was limited by her trust fund to a million dollars per year, who regularly had to borrow against the future every June.

"She's unhappy, confused, greedy, and alone," said Alex. "She's nasty and demanding and threatens to take her trust fund to another bank if we don't help her cheat the terms of her trust."

"Do you?" I asked.

"If you had my job, you'd do it too," he said.

I did not choose that moment to suggest to Alex that he was trying to accumulate a fortune that would deliver a dose of moral Thalidomide to his grandchildren in their wombs.

In the year after I worked at Slavey's, money finally reached a level of importance in my life that I found comfortable. I lived on $9,000. I went back to the place in Sawtooth Valley, remodeled a woodshed into a cabin there, and lived in it until the weather got cold. Then I bought a cheap ticket to Thailand and lived in beach shacks for three months, until the back of winter was broken. I came back and skied the Sawtooths in March and April. What jobs I held were temporary. I purchased a timber sale and sold the poles. I worked overtime on a house that was behind on a construction deadline. I taught English in a beach villa south of Bangkok to the grandchildren of rich Chinese and helped dig their BMWs out of the sand at the edge of the sea.

It was a year in which I began to remember my own life.

On the beach of Koh Phangan, an island in the Gulf of Siam, I remembered something I should never have forgotten. I remembered building fence for Bill Harrah, on his ranch on the Middle Fork of the Salmon. It was a memory that frightened me because I had forgotten it so thoroughly, and was only able to recall it when I had opted out of what passed for normal life.

The model of memory I had been proceeding on—that time creates experience and experience creates wisdom—was, at least in this instance, false. In its place was memory as quaking bog: shifting, treacherous, and perverse. I had forgotten something that would have guided me well, both in my conversations with Alex and in my teaching and my dealings with people who had more money than me. As I begin to think of life as an epic of deterioration, it's not the brittling of bones or the clogging of arteries that I focus on. It's the thought of forgetting those truths that once seemed obvious, of losing the ability to read the lessons of life.

I was sixteen when I went to work for a contractor who was building fence around Bill Harrah's ranch. Because Harrah had not been allowed to cut logs within what was then the Idaho Primitive Area, the raw materials for the fence had to come from the outside.

So we would cut logs off a timber sale ten miles north of Stanley, trailer them sixty miles downriver to the airport at Challis, peel them with drawknives and cut them to length, dip them in post-treat, and load them, 3,000 pounds at a time, into Harrah's old De Havilland Twin Otter. Then we would hop in, sit in the small jump seats in the rear of the plane, and fly up and over the mountains west of Challis. When the plane cleared the last high ridge, it would plunge down into the Middle Fork to the Thomas Creek airstrip. There we would unload the logs onto a wagon, horse-draw them to the fence line, and set up fence.

It was the first time I had ever been in an airplane. As I watched the logs float around the cabin when the plane hit air pockets, I realized I was in a different dimension of money. It was not just something you had to have to keep the bank from taking away the house or the farm. Harrah could fly whole fences into his ranch simply because he didn't want to argue with the Forest Service about cutting trees on the Middle Fork.

When I saw the ranch, I also saw that everything there, not just the fences, had been flown in on the Otter. The ranch itself was only about seventy acres, and I was told that Harrah had already spent $4 million on it. I was making $300 a month and board, and board usually turned out to be cold Franco-American spaghetti that we opened and ate out of the can out on the timber sale or in the shade of a fuel truck at the Challis airport.

Even so, I began to feel relatively wealthy when my boss hired a new man, who was wanted on auto-theft charges. My boss sent the new worker and his pregnant wife into the Middle Fork on the Otter and set them up in a tent up the canyon above Harrah's lodge. I found out the new guy was making $35 a month and groceries.

Harrah visited the ranch once while I was there. At the time he had just married one of his showgirls. A dude wrangler at the ranch reported that he spent mornings sitting in a chair on the side of the pool reading *Playboy* while his new wife, in a bikini, paddled away in front of him.

"If I was married to her," said the wrangler, "I wouldn't be sitting there looking at any damn magazine."

I spent a month flying in and out of the Middle Fork, putting up fence with a guy who wouldn't talk about his past except to say that he had worked in a lot of carnivals, and cutting timber outside of Stanley.

I was blissfully happy. I had never flown before. I had never worked with a felon before. The Middle Fork Ranch seemed to be just one more part of a world that was mine to enjoy as I wished.

At the end of the month my boss said he couldn't pay me because he didn't have any money. Harrah hadn't paid him, he said. I told him I wasn't going to work if he wasn't going to pay me, and I went back to my rented cabin in Stanley.

Harrah also had a cabin in Stanley—several of them, in fact, and a big log house in the middle of them. A few days later I heard he was in town. I walked over to his place and found him in his front yard with his bodyguard.

"Are you Bill Harrah?" I asked. He said he was. The bodyguard, a nervous man who had been a high police official in Los Angeles prior to the Miranda ruling, gave me his complete attention.

"Your contractor isn't paying me, "I said. "He says you aren't paying him."

Harrah frowned and said nothing. "We'll take care of it," said his bodyguard.

I thanked him and left. A day later I got my money.

It turned out that my boss had tricked seven or eight sixteen-year-olds into working for him for a month or two. When they quit when he didn't pay them, he went to a different town and hired someone else. He was paying on a piece of property in Montana, trying to get enough ahead to have a place of his own. He left town shortly after Harrah canceled the fence contract.

The man who was working for $35 a month ended up begging food from the Middle Fork Lodge kitchen. His wife lost her baby, there in that tent above the ranch. When I saw them again they were hitchhiking out of Stanley. I picked them up and took them twenty miles beyond my parents' place, for reasons that were not entirely generous.

Harrah soon divorced the showgirl and married Bobby Gentry the singer. That marriage also ended, about the time Gentry put a song on the charts about a tough-as-nails poor girl who uses her beauty to attain power and wealth.

The next summer I was working for the Forest Service, running a pack string down the Middle Fork, and I passed Harrah's ranch on my way to the Thomas Creek guard station. Across the river from the dusty trail I traveled were the ranch buildings, their logs stained and oiled. The grass around them was bright green and trimmed. The fences were straight and solid. The smooth water in the pool mirrored the great log lodge. No one sat in the chairs beside the water. A Model-T pickup, restored to a bright perfection, was parked on the grass on my side of the river.

And yet I did not immediately begin dreaming of having a place of my own, a place walled off from the world by mountains and a raging river, with its own hot springs and mile of

road and a restored antique Ford. The memory of that day—
the terribly important memory I had forgotten—was that I
had looked upon splendor and was not consumed by envy.

A few years later Bill Harrah died on the operating table during what was supposed to be a routine heart-bypass operation. He left behind a few hundred million dollars and a
great many employees who mourned his death. It had been
his practice to give people who were down on their luck second chances, and there were more than a few people who re-
paid their monetary debts to him with gratitude and respect.

But I have wondered if Harrah chose his death. I have a
friend who had a near-death experience during an operation
to fuse her ankle. She says that under anesthesia she could
see very clearly her circumstances: an abusive marriage, a
collapsed dream of being a dancer, and a job that allowed her
to stay a paycheck away from disaster. She also saw that she
had a choice of whether to live or die and she chose to die.
Then, remembering that she also had a child, she chose to
live. It was the most painful decision she ever made, she says.

I've wondered if Harrah, seeing clearly how cut off from
human contact his life had become, seeing his wealth for the
weight it was, didn't choose to die in the middle of his operation. Perhaps he saw, in that moment of clarity, that there
was another Eden, one not made by the hands of men.

I'm sure that Alex has *ten* million dollars by now. I'm sure
he's working on making it into a hundred million. He doesn't
talk about it much because when the subject of his wealth

comes up, I ask him for some of it. I'm teaching again, indulging in my fantasy of making the world a better place, trying to teach people self-consciousness and how to articulate the intricacies of their lives. I tell him he should do something with his money, such as fund a chair in Creative Writing here at the College of Idaho, now called Albertson College because Joe Albertson, founder of the supermarket chain, gave the place $35 million.

"No way," he says. "You don't even have a football team anymore."

"Keep your grandchildren from becoming monsters," I tell him. "Build a dorm."

"I'm going to give a million or two to Boise State University," he says. "So they can buy some more linebackers."

He says this to drive me crazy. I've told him that BSU is nothing but a support system for a semipro football team, one that will win a national championship about the time continental drift moves Boise into the middle of Nebraska.

"Don't you want to make the world a better place?" I ask.

"When you've worked with money as much as I have," he tells me, "you begin to doubt that it has the ability to make the world a better place."

"At least give a couple of farm kids scholarships," I say.

"So they can become bankers?" he asks.

There is a hint of self-loathing in his words. I have wondered if the high point of Alex's life wasn't that time when he was working forty hours a week and getting A's in high-school math class and sacking skinny quarterbacks with enough force to catch the attention of a small-college coach. Of course, I've wondered if the high point of my life wasn't when I could look at Bill Harrah's Middle Fork estate and not feel any lack or need or want within myself. Maybe we are all just trying, by whatever means we can master, to regain a childlike sense of being complete. Maybe we are all just trying not to loathe the incomplete creatures we have become.

Alex responded seriously, once, to my request for money for a good cause.

"I'll give *you* money," he said. "And you can give it to anybody you want. You can keep it. You can throw it away. You can buy lottery tickets with it." And he wrote a check for a $100,000 and handed it to me.

I handed it back. It reminded me of something Alex had said when I had asked him for money the first time.

"You don't know what I've had to do for my money," he said. "I've had to trade my whole life for it. If I give it to somebody else I'll be giving them free time. I'd rather keep my money and have them know I *could* give them free time, but I won't. It's the only way I get their attention."

At the time I thought he was kidding, but after having that check in my hand, I wasn't so sure. My good intentions, my desire to help poor farm kids get an education, and even my desire to go back to Thailand and spend a year on the beach all melted into the giddy, dizzying feeling of having taken a drug so new that I hadn't known I had receptors for it. I had a sudden sensation of having a whole new set of fantasies to explore, and those fantasies had to do with other people and what they would do for a little free time. While in Thailand I had been disgusted by the sight of rich Europeans, Arabs, and Japanese leading entourages of child whores into their hotels, but it dawned on me that being rich in America could be a variation of the same transaction.

Lately Alex has been asking me to keep an eye out for property in Sawtooth Valley. He's again talking about retirement, but every time I come up with a property I think would make a nice place to retire to, he scrutinizes it for investment potential and rejects it. I cut him no slack when this happens. I tell him that he can't see the world for its price tags, but it doesn't seem to bother him.

"Keep looking," he says. "I don't want to be standing on a place that's losing value."

*On the north side of the island of Maui is a beach where every af-
ternoon the winds get high and steady and the waves get enormous.
If you stand at the top of the steep slope that separates the beach
from the Hana Highway, you can watch fifty or a hundred bright
sails among the waves. It looks like a rest stop on a butterfly mi-
gration, or would if butterflies rested on water and came with
glowing twelve-foot wings.*

*Standing there on solid ground, you can watch windsurfers do
front flips and 360s with gear that looks impossibly cumbersome
and flimsy. In high winds, they balance on the crashing crests of
waves for what seems like minutes. And if they fall off their
boards, it only takes them a few seconds to hook the wind with their
sails, pull themselves upright, and fly over the waves again.*

*I've been staying in a house a few miles from the beach. On my
way into Paia, the nearest town with a grocery store and a post office, I've stopped to watch the windsurfers dance. I've wondered
how long it would take to sell everything I own, pick up a used*

board and a quiver of sails, travel back to Maui, and find a Paia night job. The man who runs the rental shop says that if I took lessons and windsurfed every day for a year, I wouldn't be a complete incompetent every time I got near a sail and a board.

I've taken one lesson so far. Complete incompetent is much too mild a term for me. In spite of having a board only a little smaller than a gillnetter, I have fallen off it one way and then the other for two hours. The mast has fallen on my head, the sail has trapped me under water, and I have dozens of small deep cuts in the soles of my feet from landing on coral in the shallow waters of the bunny bay. Through the pain, I've been thinking of how to get that year or two or three away from job and home so I can learn to windsurf like they windsurf on the north side of Maui.

Maybe three years wouldn't be enough. Five years, I tell myself. In five years I could work into a really good night job in Paia, like bartending.

But five years is a long time to take direction. It's a long time to expect frontal lobes to survive the crash of forehead against fiberglass at every misjudged wave.

It's a long time to stay in the sun, too. My windsurfing instructor, who is maybe thirty, has a sun-ulcered face. The skin on his back looks like the fine Corinthian leather we once heard about in Chrysler ads. He'll end up as a headrest in a convertible if he's not careful how he fills out his organ donor card.

Across a narrow isthmus from Paia, on the southwest side of Maui, is a great Hotel, a structure that could take first place among the Seven Wonders of the World of Dubious Japanese Financing. It's rumored to have cost $700 million, which means its $500-a-night rooms need to be constantly occupied or the place will return its in-

vestment about the time Captain Janeway assumes command of the Starship Voyager.

The Hotel is no Motel 6. The restrooms have more marble and gilt-framed mirrors than the Hermitage. Fat bronze sculptures of nude women lounge about the marble-columned atrium. Out on the beach, a river courses down through house-sized blocks of frozen lava, spilling into a series of waterfalls and pools, pools and waterfalls. Palm trees and flowers line its banks, and it flows down toward the beach until it hits one final pool. Then it's pumped back up to the top again. It's an elaborate and enormous waterslide, crafted to look like one of the wild basalt canyons that spill off the rainy side of Maui's volcano.

But there are no rough edges in this basalt canyon. People float by, hanging on to short sections of log that upon inspection reveal themselves to be molded chunks of plastic foam. Even the great rocks are hollow concrete, textured and painted to look like basalt. Walk through an artificial cave in one of these artificial rocks, and you'll hear the whining of vast machinery. Deep beneath the Hotel there must be an entire city of Morlocks.

On the surface, however, everything a guest could possibly touch has been groomed. Even the water off the beach is, in effect, groomed by flags designating when it's safe to be in it. If there's a storm or a shark scare, different flags come out and they won't let you go into the water.

Much of Maui's shoreline has been groomed in similar ways. Walk along the beach in front of any of the grand hotels and you'll find landscaping crews working on bermed flower beds, clipping lawns to putting-green tolerances, or polishing up sculptures. One of the measures of luxury in the hotel business is the ratio of staff to guests. Four staff members for every guest is not out of the question at places like the Hotel.

Each guest's experience is planned in advance. The Hotel's financial and human resources have been devoted to sanding and smoothing that experience into a series of expected transactions. It gives rise to an irrational fear that heaven will be expensive to visit and that when you've ridden all the rides there, bought all your souvenirs, and maxed out all your credit cards, they'll kick you out.

So who are the people paying $500 a night to stay here? Who's putting fingerprints on the great bronze breasts of the sculptures, drinking mai-tais in front of the hula dancers on the lawn, and sliding down the smooth waterfalls, plastic logs in their arms? They're not Indonesian generals, corrupt televangelists and their exotic mistresses, or members of old European banking families. They're American professionals—people with jobs, consuming jobs, jobs that pay them enviable salaries, plus stock options and year-end bonuses.

But these are also people who are at poverty level in terms of time. They work seventy or eighty or ninety hours a week in those jobs, and then they get two weeks off before doing it all over for another year.

Such people don't want surprises on their vacations. They can afford to spend a great deal—in fact, how much they spend is a measure of the quality of their time away from work. They don't want to be excited. Many of them are in service industries themselves, and part of the reason they go on vacation is to be on the happy end of the human transaction they know best.

The Hotel deals with a clientele that demands not just illusion and not just anesthesia, but the anesthesia of illusion. It's no secret that the native Hawaiians who stand on the artificial rocks every evening and chant to Hawaiian gods all have day jobs. But that doesn't matter. What matters is the painstaking construction of a seamless surface that mirrors the hastily erected dreams of someone who has to spend lots of money in not very much time.

That said, the dream that I see in the reflective surface of the Hotel is of a figure in silhouette, black against the lurid red and orange and blue of a Maui sunset. He lives on the bright line between the air and the waves, and he dances there, and the sunset makes his sail into a great candle, and the warm air wraps around him and where he touches the water there's a pool of light.

His internal surfaces are as carefully textured as those in any grand hotel. His reflexes are as smooth as any burnished sculpture in any marbled atrium, and if free time represents unattainable wealth to all those doctors and lawyers and middle managers sitting around the waterslide drinking mai-tais, he has spent an impossible fortune on them. He's not even looking to get that investment back.

Skiing Volcanoes

W<small>E WERE ON</small> Mount Lassen, a half-mile up the slope above the lodge, when I stepped out onto a small cornice and kicked off its curl with my lower ski. An avalanche started below me. It sounded like concrete pouring into a bathtub. It rushed down 100 yards to the top of a knoll, where it piled into a soggy, neck-deep pyramid. I looked at my ski partner, Sean Petersen, and then at the steep slope we were about to climb. Between us and the summit of Lassen were avalanches-in-waiting, ones far bigger than the one I'd just triggered.

And it was pouring rain. Already the top six inches of a fifteen-foot snowpack had turned to slush. Thick fog was drifting down through slide-trimmed trees and cascading over basalt cliffs, making getting back to the car a matter of not losing sight of our tracks.

Sean shrugged. "Nobody said it would be easy."

"Nobody said it would be lucky, either," I said. "Let's get out of here. If I'm going to die, I'd rather die on Shasta."

Skiing back to the car, I kicked off another avalanche coming off a turn and twice burrowed into drifts with my ski tips, discovering what it feels like to swan-dive into a Slurpee. Sean was skiing cautiously, hugging the trees, but he was turning both ways. This was good news.

Sean is my only famous friend, and he's famous only because of a photo in a Patagonia ad. In the photo, Sean is silhouetted between two great rocks that frame a chasm. His hands are braced against rock and his feet hang in big air. The ad copy reads, "Sean Petersen taking a bouldering break . . . on the border of Nepal and Tibet." The photo gives a small thrill of wonder, and what you wonder is, "How's he gonna get down?" Sean says it was easier than it looks.

Within a year, Sean found himself trying to get down from a place where nothing was easy. He was leading a climb up the Elephant's Perch, a perpendicular face in Idaho's Sawtooth Range, when rocks fell from above, cracking his skull in a long, ragged line above his right ear. He was carried down unconscious, first by other climbers and then by helicopter. When I saw his CAT scans, I couldn't understand how he had survived. His temporal lobes were full of blood, indicating that he had been hit hard enough on one side of his skull to smash his brain against the other side. He was thirty-three years old.

After a week he came out of the coma. After a month he was able to take brief walks. After three months he was home and beginning to go on wobbly runs. He had been a chef, but the first work he was able to do was shoveling snow off roofs near his home in Sun Valley—a combination of job and therapy, as long as he didn't fall off.

His balance wasn't good. He talked like a computer with bad software. He couldn't hear well out of one ear. He'd forgotten how to play the guitar. But when he went back to the hospital for a checkup his neurosurgeon looked at him with awe.

"You're not supposed to be alive," said the neurosurgeon. "And stay off those roofs."

His skull had been broken in August. Now he was my ski partner, and it was the first week in May.

It was not our first volcano tour. Eight years earlier, we had started out to climb and ski Lassen, Shasta, McGloughlin, Hood, and St. Helens. One a day.

We almost made it. We stopped at the Pole, Pedal, and Paddle celebration in Bend, Oregon, for a day, seduced off-task by street music and the local microbrews. But at the end of six days, we'd climbed and skied the five volcanoes.

On Hood, we'd skied past a line of climbers, roped together for safety, and laughed at their mutterings as we caught air off the cornices they struggled up. On St. Helens, we'd danced on the edge of the world and watched the oozing lava dome through holes in the mist below. We'd gotten lost in fog on Shasta but had found a gap in the Red Banks to ski down, and had skied McGloughlin in near-darkness because we'd stayed on its summit to watch the sun set. Lassen had been a giant sunlit amusement-park ride of corn snow and rounded knolls.

But eight years can change more than the weather, even when they don't include climbing accidents. As a ski partner, I too had drawbacks. One was that I'd been a sedentary English professor long enough to get out of shape. I'd also *lived* long enough to get out of shape. We had only gone a half-mile up Lassen, but my skis had felt heavy and my breath had come hard. My face, sun-bronzed when I had worked on the Sun Valley ski patrol, now bore the marks of my dermatologist's spray can of liquid nitrogen. I was still complaining when we got into the car. "The best thing about sports where the experts die," I said, "is that you don't have to worry about what comes after you finish being expert."

The rain was already in Shasta City when we got there. We went into town for dinner and ended the evening shooting pool in a saloon. Sean's neurologist didn't want him to drink alcohol, so we drank near-beer, to the disgust of the bartender and the amusement of the biker crowd hanging out at the front of the bar.

The trouble with mountains is that they won't stay climbed. They don't usually change that much, and you do. Sooner or later you look up at a summit and realize that *you* haven't ever been there.

We were on Shasta's Rabbit Flats at six-forty-five in the morning. Late. The sky was clear and the snow was rock-hard, but at that time of year it could all be slush by afternoon. We tried hard not to look at the summit, some 7,200 vertical feet away.

With telemark skis, three-pin bindings, lightweight boots, skins, and bullet-proof snow, you can climb far faster than you can with hiking boots and bare rock. So our first 3,000 vertical feet on Shasta, which got us to Helen Lake—the overnight bivouac for climbers who take two days to ascend the south side—went quickly and far more easily than our trek up Lassen.

But then, in upper Avalanche Bowl, the slope steepened to forty degrees. We had to keep our skis heading straight up the fall line. To move off vertical and set an edge meant an uncontrollable slide back down the mountain, maybe for minutes.

We headed for the Red Banks and found the couloir we had once skied down. It was lined with ice but enough snow had drifted in that we could kick steps for 100 yards to where the slope leveled off just before Misery Hill.

It was a new climate zone. The sun disappeared behind the lenticular cloud that had begun forming on Shasta's summit. The temperature dropped below freezing. The snow changed to pure rime, marbled with ice. Wind currents, carrying glittering golden crystals, snapped into sudden visibility. We were above 12,000 feet and it was becoming hard to breathe, harder still to put one boot in front of the other. At the base of Misery Hill we stopped to have lunch.

Suddenly we had company. Two figures moved up the slope toward us, covering ground far faster than we had. A man and a woman, both in their mid-twenties, stopped at our resting place. They were from Colorado and were, like us, climbing and skiing peaks. They were just doing it a lot faster. The man introduced himself as Flash. They put on their windsuits and moved on up the hill, leaving us behind.

"They're going to beat us to the top," I said.

"Relax," said Sean. "We're eight years ahead of them."

"Now I know why old men send young men off to war."

"You were like that twenty years ago."

"I didn't call myself Flash," I said.

The temporal lobes are where a lot of what we call personality resides. When Sean was in a coma, there was uncertainty about who he'd wake up as: Sean or Elvis. But when he did wake up he started recognizing people and acting like himself, mostly.

That's not to say there haven't been changes. Sean no longer has that brain function that allows the polite evasions and lies that allow us to exist as a social species. He's more honest than anybody I know.

The drill on Misery Hill was, first, a hundred steps, stop, breathe. Then fifty steps, stop, breathe. Then fifty steps, stop, breathe fifty times. Then breathe a hundred times and take fifty steps if possible.

I was following Sean up the mountain when he turned around and said, "You've got this whole mountain to choose a route from. Go over there and climb. Stay out of my tracks."

I went. I didn't have the breath to argue. He was right, anyway. Even with a mile of its vertical below us, Shasta was still a big mountain. I was thinking that Sean had the sort of personal boundaries now that would save him expensive years of psychotherapy, but I was in no mood to cheer him up by telling him that.

We went deeper into the cloud that balanced on the summit. At the top of Misery Hill we stumbled upward in thick fog, following the tracks of climbers we hoped knew where they were going. Oxygen deprivation, leg spasms, fatigue, and a near-beer hangover combined to put us in a state of unworldly and breathless pain.

We struggled along the summit plateau and past the steaming hot spots that we knew were close to the end of our journey. Finally, on top of Shasta, we found Flash and Ms. Flash, who looked us over with surprise. We were bug-eyed and sucking air, suffering from altitude sickness, exercise sickness, and how-did-we-get-here sickness, but we had made it. Now all we had to do was get down.

Thirty-six hours later, we were sitting in the dining room of Mount Hood's Timberline Lodge, looking down at a dinner of veal and morel mushrooms. The lodge was offering lodging and dinner in the dining room for $50 a person. Life was good. Life was especially good because we had made it off Shasta.

We had spent a long half hour in dreamy lassitude on Shasta's summit, drinking all our Gatorade and finally understanding why they find smiling dead climbers on top of peaks. Then, skis on, we traversed down through what we hadn't noticed on the way up: a weird dreamscape of drifts and monoliths and wind-shattered boulders that led to the top of Misery. Going down, Misery is a gentle slope. In fact, it's the world's highest bunny hill, except for the cliffs between it and the parking lot.

The day's warmth had finally begun to soften Shasta's snow. When we'd climbed back down through the Red Banks, our skis sank deep into supremely soggy stuff. Small avalanches were coming down the sides of Avalanche Bowl.

Flash and Ms. Flash had descended a long, terrifyingly steep couloir a crucial twenty minutes earlier, leaving perfect tracks.

I got halfway down the bowl without setting anything off, but when the slush got to my knees, my strength and skiing skills left me. A final fast and out-of-control emergency turn ended when I arrowed into a cornice and pitched headfirst into a mixture of water and ice cubes. My pack, briefly airborne, came down on my head.

It took me a while to get to my feet. My legs were shaking with fatigue and I was hurting all over. I was bleeding from my forehead. Below me, Sean was making nice, round, careful, slow-motion telemark turns.

With 3,000 vertical feet to go, I began traversing a half-mile, doing a kick turn, then traversing another half-mile. By the time I got to the parking lot, I had seen as much of Shasta as it's possible to see in fifteen giant traverses. I'd fallen on my face again, dodged slow-moving avalanches, and whenever I'd tried to hop around a turn, my knees had collapsed. Blood and sweat were seeping into my eyes. My legs were shaking and I walked with a stoop and a shuffle across the asphalt to the car. Flash, sitting in the midst of gear spread out on the parking lot to dry, looked at me with amusement. I snarled at him. I was living proof that you can climb and ski a 14,000-foot peak in a day and end up feeling humiliated and disgusted with yourself.

We skipped McGloughlin. Seeing it across Klamath Lake from the highway, we made the decision quickly. Neither of us was in any shape to climb its sharp summit, even if it was only 9,500 feet high. We stayed in Bend that night, sleeping well on painkillers left over from Sean's rehab.

At Timberline Lodge, the following night, I woke at four in the morning, scared. Shasta was more worrisome in retrospect than it had been up close. We had descended a half hour later than we should have, and if we'd been a half hour later than that, the fragile bond between two layers of snow might have broken. We'd had a contingency plan—to ski the paths avalanches had already taken—if Avalanche Bowl was living up to its name when we skied it. But it's not good to have contingency plans like that.

And the last time we'd been on the top of Hood, somebody below started screaming, "Falling!" At the head of the narrow couloir that leads to Hood's summit, a climber had tipped backward and tumbled, taking a half-dozen roped-up novices for a short slide down the hogback below. I hadn't thought about it much since, but after Shasta, their screams had begun to resonate.

The world, of course, is more frightening at four in the morning than it is in daylight.

We were on top of Hood, in bright sun, at ten that morning. We could see the damaged peak of St. Helens, our next destination, through forty miles of clear air.

After Shasta, Hood had been a walk, although the frost was five feet thick on the rocks near the top, and I was hoping the warmth of the morning didn't loosen it. The couloir at the top was safe if you took it slow and made sure of your footing.

Last time, we had carried our skis past one of the roped-up climbers, who said, "I've seen a lot of people pack skis up this mountain. But they all pack them back down."

So we had taken them to the high headwall that marks the summit and skied down, in deep and shifting powder, past him.

This time we were alone. It was a good thing, because the snow was so icy it was difficult to keep a ski on it. Falling was not an option.

Sean skied down to Hood's hot spots in long careful traverses. I hopped one way, did a chattering sideslip for a hundred feet, hopped the other way, and chattered again. It was only below the hot spots that we got into corn snow.

Suddenly I could ski. The boards on my feet were no longer just a dangerous pair of snowshoes. My thighs suddenly had muscle tone. We skied the broad bowl of the White Salmon Glacier, shot over the snow bridges that spanned its crevasses, and made figure eights down to the open, broad face of Hood's ski area, where I harassed snowboarders and Sean practiced his telemark wedeln.

We got to Cougar, Washington, in time for a giant burger at a local tavern, which in one sitting restored all the calories we'd burned so far. Then we rented a cabin in a small mom-and-pop resort. The air was warm, the wide lawns were deep green and dotted with picnic tables, and the entire valley was basking in the first really warm day of summer. It reminded me of long-ago warm seasons, when school was out, jobs were for grownups, and adventure could be had for the price of walking out the door.

"Is it bad to relive your adolescence?" I asked Sean.

He thought for a moment. "We never got out of adolescence." he said. He grinned. "I'm lucky I'm not skiing with a walker. That's what I think about on days like this."

It was barely light the next morning when we began the long approach to St. Helens. Heavy drifts still blocked the closest approach to the summit, so we were on the June Lake trail or lava fields for the first three miles, skis on our shoulders, sandals on our feet. When we finally hit snow, we put on our skis and skins. Four hours and 5,600 vertical feet later, we arrived at the crater's lip.

Sean wanted me to go way out on the cornice for a picture, but I wouldn't do it. The lava dome wasn't oozing anymore, but steam was coming off it and it didn't look like hospitable terrain. Around the rim, a constant loud rockfall called attention to loosely structured overhangs. I wondered how much air there was beneath our feet.

We worried about softening snow. After ten minutes we started down. Things got happily out of control within seconds.

The snow on the top of St. Helens had been melted, by sun and ash, into a forest of tiny six-inch ice trees. Skiing through them created a music-box tinkling that turned into a chorus of ecstatic voices whenever we set a fast edge. A few hundred weightless, wondrously effortless turns farther down, we hit slopes that had been darkened by windblown ash, and our tracks became neon white on a background of gray and brown and black. We got on a long finger of snow—two inches of corn on a hard base—and inscribed a tangle of tracks on its bowls and knolls to within a few hundred feet of June Lake. The walk out wasn't bad. We were almost sorry to see the car.

Somewhere around Hood River, cruising in the fast lane on I-84, a half-rack of O'Doul's on the seat between us, I scrabbled through the tape box for Neil Young's *Rust Never Sleeps.* Sean wanted to listen to bluegrass, though, and it was his tape deck. It was okay. I was feeling younger than I had felt a week before.

I had my reasons. On Hood, skiing under Steel Cliff, I was astonished by the ringing of thousands of tiny cinders as they fell from the cliff face. A hundred thousand years of cinders raining down, I thought, and Hood would be short and stumpy. By then, a new mountain would have taken its place. I wondered if mountains, even though their lifetimes are immeasurably longer than ours, have midlife crises. Maybe that's what explosive eruptions are all about.

At a rest stop in central Oregon, we cleaned the corn chips, bean dip, and beer bottles out of the car and totted up expenses. We had spent $500 and a precious week of our lives to climb 18,000 vertical feet and come back down.

It seemed worth it. Because even if I remained in a world whose central principle was entropy, I found myself happier than I had been since I'd turned forty. Even if mountains don't heal, I was thinking, people do.

*Across the highway from my house is a big sagebrush-covered hill,
one composed of soft granite sand piled into a big bullet shape 800
feet high and many degrees steeper than the angle of repose. There
are days I suspect that a good earthquake might bring it down
across the road and onto my roof, which wasn't designed for such
loads.*

*Even on days when earthquakes don't seem likely, it is hard to
forget that the hill is there. In the mornings, I stay in its shadow
for an hour while the rest of the valley greets the sunrise. In the
winters it holds the snow until a warm storm drops a foot or two of
wet powder on a drier, looser base—then all the snow, wet and dry,
comes sliding down and crashing through our eastern fences. The
children of summer visitors climb the hill and get lost on its back-
side. Armies of venison-crazed hunters attack it every opening day.
Lightning is attracted to it and dish-rattling thunder comes
quickly after the flash of every hilltop bolt.*

I like having a hill in my backyard, especially a big and steep one. Over the years I've worn a trail to its summit. I've sat up there and watched the sun go down over the Sawtooths, wandered with deer and coyotes through the trees on the hill's northern face, and smashed Olympic long-jump records in its sliding sands. I've even enjoyed repairing the fences in the spring. If the hill were suddenly gone, I would feel a loss far beyond that represented by an hour of sleep in the mornings.

With typical human vanity, I tell myself the hill has become a part of me. But someone watching me as I run up it on a summer day, blinded by sweat and gasping for air, unable to think, conscious only of the smell of warm rock and sage and the pain of lungs and thighs—that someone would surely say that I have become a part of the hill.

Winter mornings find me struggling into polypropylene under-wear and ski clothes, pressing climbing skins to the bottom of my telemark skis, walking across the road, and beginning the long trek to the hilltop. It is my daily constitutional, and I try to climb the 800 vertical feet at a steady pace, even on the steeper parts of my track.

The prevailing winter winds blow down the valley, south to north, so I climb the southern ridge. It is wind-packed and corniced all the way to the top, and climbing it is like walking up a long frozen sidewalk. At the very top, even after heavy snow storms, the winds leave the ground bare. The vegetation is twisted and small. Once, just for the novelty of touching stone in the middle of a deep-snow winter, I pried a rock out of the small cairn on the hilltop. Under it were thousands of ladybugs, huddled in rows, waiting for spring. I replaced the rock gently, with the embarrassment, say, of a god who has lifted the roof off a church not dedicated to his own worship.

It is dangerous to ski the hill's west face, owing to its steepness and the big windslabs that build up in its gullies. Even in the spring, when avalanches are less of a danger, you can hook your elbows on the snow as you finish a turn there, and a fall can mean an accelerating headfirst slide into whatever has melted out of the drifts at the bottom.

But the north ridge, half-timbered and half-sage, has a fall line just right for big sweeping turns. The snow that blows from the south drifts in here, and even when it hasn't snowed for days there's fresh powder in among the trees. On good days I can get fifty turns in on the trip down to the highway. On good days I do a couple of constitutionals.

When my family first bought the ranch we would visit it in the winters, even though we couldn't live here. None of the cabins were insulated against winter temperatures, and besides, there wasn't anything to do even if you could stay warm.

But on weekends, we would drive up to check on the place, and I remember wandering through a darkened, snow-buried-house, looking with wonder at the shattered remains of water glasses left carelessly full of water, or at the frost filigrees on the stoves, or at snow tracked in a month earlier, still fresh on the linoleum. I was all of five, six, seven, and eight. On one of these trips I brought along that year's Christmas present, a pair of wooden skis with a Nordic ski jumper in full flight embossed on each tip. I didn't have poles, and the skis were fastened to my rubber overshoes with single wide leather straps that went over my insteps. We stopped at the ranch, but only briefly, and then went on to the town of Stanley to visit friends. It was a sunny day, if a cold one, and I was left outside to try out my new skis while the older folks sat around a stove and caught up on the Stanley news.

The hill on the south edge of town, before it came to be covered with houses, used to grow a large wind curl of snow, eight feet high in places, and it was toward this structure that I set off. Somebody had taught me how to herringbone, and I slowly made my way up the slope, following the bright promise drawn so vividly on my ski tips.

It wasn't hard to get around the wind curl, and once above it, I found that the slope flattened considerably. I didn't want to go off the jump at high speed, at least not at first, so when I turned around and my skis began to slide, I was glad not to be going down too steep an approach. Still, by the time I hit the edge, my skis were singing soprano against the crust, and I experienced a small bit of doubt as I found myself launched out into an immensity of air.

There was a long moment of regret, during which I tried to pose as a Nordic jumper, forward-leaning, hands held against hips, supremely confident. Then there was a loud crunch as I hit headfirst and stuck.

I was able to kick off my skis and somehow wriggle my way back up to the surface of the snow before I suffocated. My face was cold and skinned, and the first streaks of blood against the snow sent me into a panic. I ran back to the house my parents were visiting, where I was taken in and comforted, and from where my father later emerged to rescue my abandoned skis.

Coming back into my house these days, pulling off my ski boots, shaking the snow out of my collar, and reaching for whatever coffee is left in the pot, I find myself remembering that first jump. I remember its sensate shocks: the sudden nothing beneath my feet, the discrete intense sun that day, the sharply tilted postcard vision of Stanley rising toward me. I remember the wind—its noise and its invasive touch and shifting forms, revealed in cornice and spin-drift. And most of all the feeling of flight. This, across forty-five winters.

And if I fail to make the connections, sitting in a place where a cold bright wind sculpts the snow, where my skis lean against the front-porch rail, and where once a day, if I climb a hill, I can fly, it's only because I'm not completely ready to give up the idea of my own free will. I'm not fully able to wonder if there isn't, with me and maybe with everybody else, some early experience for which all sub-sequent living is merely repetition and elaboration. I'm not sure if I can accept what happened to me that day, when I must have be-come indentured to these hills.

That's on days that threaten earthquakes. On good days, though, I can embrace it all. On good days I know that I don't have free will. Probably nobody raised in Sawtooth Valley does. But that's okay. We have free fall.

Traplines

MY FATHER REMAINED a trapper all his life. Even when he had retired from his traplines, he saw animal tracks with a trapper's eyes, watched the willows along the Salmon River behind his house for the fresh tooth marks of beaver, and checked the price of fur when a fur-buying house sent him one of their infrequent bulletins. The price of fur has been poor for decades now, so my father had less incentive to dream of his trapping days, when he was able to take Septembers, Octobers, and Novembers off from salaried jobs to walk the stream banks and logging roads of Sawtooth Valley and still make enough money to support a family.

He wasn't bothered by the innocent young men who once sought him out as a mentor. They would ask him to teach them to trap and he would tell them where and how to make sets for beaver, muskrat, bobcat, and coyote. He would skin and stretch what they caught and split the profits with them. Such partnerships usually only lasted a season or two, until the young men realized that the life they wanted to live was best lived in a different century and that the reason my father had been able to make life as a trapper practical was because he had other irons in the fire, sometimes literally: he has also been a welder, a blacksmith, and a mechanic.

But he remained a trapper. He trapped mice on his back porch and the moles that punctured his lawn in the summer. He picked out spots where a trap could be concealed beneath the small paths made by mink along the river, and he spotted the coyotes as they walked the hills around his house. At some level of memory, he wanted to trap those coyotes, kill them, take them home and skin them, and stretch their hides to dry over frames until the fur buyer came through.

You would think that such desire would have alienated him from the complex and not-human world that begins beyond our family's fence lines in Sawtooth Valley, but it didn't. Near the end of his active trapping career, he spread a few traps along the trail on the other side of the river one fall and then watched as a storm covered them with two feet of snow. He left the traps there over the winter, and it wasn't until the next July, when he was out wandering his pastures, that he thought to check them. He crossed the river and gathered them up, all of them snow sprung except one, which held a young coyote, fresh caught, in the trap for only minutes. Because it was summer and the coyote was small, its fur worthless to the buyers, he put a pine branch across its neck, pinned it to the ground, released its leg from the trap, and stepped back to watch it run off.

I asked him what the coyote had looked like. "Happy," he

said. But there was more to it than happy. He knew he had been called into a world that the coyotes usually keep for themselves. That was the last time my father put out traps for any animal that didn't irritate him.

I don't trap. I grew up with trapping and hunting smells rising up from the cellar of our house: the sharp odors of stripped flesh and clotted blood, gutted ducks and pheasants, beaver scent glands, and the rancid piles of fat scraped from hides. As a small child, when I had accompanied my father on his traplines, we had often come upon mink and marten and otter alive in his traps. I wanted to take them home as pets. They would hiss and scream and tear at the earth at the end of their chains. Then my father would kill them. I would make a fuss, and then I'd end up sitting in the pickup while he checked more traps.

I knew they were vicious little animals and they had shown their prey no more compassion than my father showed them, but at age six it was tough to balance that knowledge against the Disney movies I had seen on a cousin's TV in Boise. Recently, when I read in a student paper the words "This story reminds me again that character is always shaped by cruel forces," I paused in my correcting for a moment and thought for the first time in months about that trapline.

My father tried to teach me to skin animals but I was awkward with the knife. I sliced through the delicate hides or tore the fur on the wooden stretchers, eliminating not just traplines but medical school from my future. He had earlier tried to teach me to hunt, with more success. I had done well at that, killing probably sixteen deer by the time I was four-teen, at which point I didn't kill anymore until I was thirty-nine.

At that advanced age, I consciously accepted my family's ethic that you ought to kill the meat you eat and began kill-ing deer and elk again. But there had been twenty-odd years in which I hadn't been very conscious of my father's trapping or hunting, even though I had eaten a lot of venison chops and elk steak in that time and had begun wearing—and still wear—a fur hat that my father gave me. It had been made from a beaver he had trapped. Once when a picture of that hat on my head showed up on the front page of a news-paper—I had been standing in an unemployment line—a woman wrote me a bitter letter about the cruelty of wearing fur. I thought about the complicated reply I would have to give her, one that would have to detail my family finances along with my family's values, and let her letter go unan-swered.

But I did begin killing again. And the act of sighting a deer's ear through a rifle scope, putting the crosshairs on it, and pulling the trigger marked me as someone who had awak-ened, not just to a paradoxical combination of ethical itch and bloodlust, but to the world I stood on. It was not an awakening caused by the roar of my rifle or the sudden high pirouette of a head-shot buck. It was caused by something else altogether.

Just before my thirty-ninth birthday I took one of the small sheds on the ranch, put it on a trailer, and wheeled it out near the river. I put it on stilts, insulated it with four inches of Styrofoam in the floors and ceiling, and equipped it with a barrel stove that my father had welded up for me. When I was done I had created a heavy-duty, industrial-model sauna.

While I was cleaning that shed out before moving it, I pried a piece of Sheetrock from one of the inside walls and discovered, hanging on nails, a cache of beaver scent glands left over from my father's trapping days. He had sold ones like them to perfume companies for tens of dollars a pound in the early sixties. Of course, it took many beaver to make a pound of scent glands, but over most of his seasons he caught ninety or a hundred of them, so scent glands had amounted to an appreciable portion of his trapping income over the years.

These, however, had been walled up and forgotten. Altogether, they made less than a pound. They were completely mummified, and the fragrant oil they had contained had sunk deep into the wood behind them. I took them off their nails and threw them onto the burning pile and a week later they were smoke.

I had paneled the inside of the sauna with cedar and built benches against the wall on either side of the stove. My girlfriend at the time was a psychotherapist, into archetypes and aromatherapy, and she brought two bunches of eucalyptus leaves, which hung from the ceiling above the stove. It was a cold day in November when we fired up the sauna for the first time. When the barrel stove was red-hot, I poured water from a bucket onto the bare metal. Great clouds of steam and eucalyptus oil began to bathe our bodies. Our sinuses snapped open. Within a few minutes, the candle in a wall mount had slumped over from the heat, and a thermometer near the roof read 160°F. A few minutes after that we dove out the door and into the Salmon River, where we stayed until heatstroke and eucalyptus overdose were no longer possibilities.

When we went back into the sauna to warm up again, we discovered a new smell. The heat had penetrated four inches of Styrofoam and volatilized the violent pheromones of the mummified rodent glands. A thick miasma of eau de beaver, sharpened by the odors of wet fresh cedar, eucalyptus, and sweat, all of it nearly too hot to breathe, was what passed for atmosphere in that sauna.

It was not unpleasant. It was the smell of home, of place, of where my heart was.

On my thirty-ninth birthday I climbed the hill behind my house and jumped a little two-point buck out of the sagebrush meadow near its summit. He ran north, down a ridge covered with thick forest and deadfall. I ran hard after him, following the sprays of soil fanning out from deep hoofprints. When I got to the bottom of the hill I could see him running over a low rise some 400 yards away. It was a long shot, and I was desperately trying to breathe and keep him in sight through the scope at the same time. I put the crosshairs between the top tines of his antlers, and as I fired, the buck jumped and met the bullet with his head.

He turned sideways in midair, fell backward, and disappeared down a short steep slope. I found him half-hidden below the low branches of sagebrush.

I had a license this time and a tag. I notched the tag and attached it to his antlers, then gutted him quickly and dragged him downhill. When I got him near a small side road that parallels the highway below my parents' house, I walked back and got the old pickup we use for hauling wood. I drove down to him, loaded him in the back, and took him back to the clothesline posts in their backyard. I hung him where I could reach him with a hose, and had just finished washing out his body cavity when my parents drove home. My father went in the house to change clothes so he could help me skin the carcass, but by the time he was back out I had finished. It was just dark when I was done with the deer.

Only then did I see that everything had gone right, and quickly.

It was not long after I had killed that deer that my relationship with the psychotherapist—who had smelled creatures in the sauna who lurked beyond her own psychic and olfactory fence lines—ended.

Out of these developments came others. I married a woman who grew up on a cattle ranch, who breathed air that carried the heavy scents of branded and castrated and butchered cows. I suspect we were brought together by our nasal receptors.

I had a few last good years of hunting with my father, and in the middle of them he told me a story then that I hadn't heard before about his years as a hardrock miner in the Triumph Mine on the East Fork of Wood River, near Ketchum. He wouldn't have thought of it as a hunting story, but I do.

The central shaft of the Triumph Mine was 1,500 feet

deep, with tunnels coming off it at right angles every 100 feet or so. Miners rode to and from the tunnels on a fenced platform suspended over the shaft by a cable and four guy wires. A windlass operator at the top lowered or raised the cable according to instructions telephoned from the mouths of the tunnels. A platform full of men would be lowered down at the beginning of a shift and raised up at the end.

It may have been that the one man riding the platform down that day was catching up with his shift partners. It may have been that he was not part of a mucking or blasting crew and was going down to work on the electrical lines or on pumps. In any case, one of the crews had carried a pile of steel rails a little too close to the shaft at the 400-foot level, and one of the rails had been pushed out farther than the rest, into the path of the platform. When the platform was lowered, it caught on that rail and tipped its lone passenger out over the fence, and into thin darkness.

My father and another man were detailed to go find him. There had been a jerk against the cable when the tipped platform had righted itself, and when no one had called up to the windlass operator, they had a good idea of what had happened. Mining stopped. Men coming onto the evening shift stood at the top of the shaft and watched as the platform, its fence torn off by the rail, came back to the surface. They watched as it descended once again, carrying my father and another miner.

At the 400-foot level they stopped and jumped into the tunnel mouth and moved the steel, and then went down level by level, stopping at each tunnel and turning on lights and shouting, then reboarding the platform. Five hundred feet farther down they gave up hope, and told the windlass operator to take them to the bottom.

"We found him huddled up, like he was cold, at the bottom of the shaft," my father told me. "He didn't look broken. He looked shrunken."

"I've seen that," I said. When I was a ski patrolman, I took the bodies of two skiers—one the victim of an avalanche, and one of a tree—down in a sled. They were too small for their clothes. Then when my friend Sean Petersen was in a coma for ten days, there was no mistaking that he had become small in the same way, lying there in the hospital bed. When he came to life again, he wasn't so small anymore.

At the bottom of the mine, they loaded the body onto the platform and rode up with it. At the surface, it was dark. My father said that the first thing that he noticed at the surface were the stars.

Those stars and the shapes they made are the same shapes he must have seen coming back across the river with a poached deer or elk lying over the saddle of his horse. The steady breathing of a large animal must have seemed a comfort, and the darkness must have held a softness it never held in the Triumph Mine. Once when I was seventeen I went to look for a job at a small and failing mine in the hills south of Hailey, and when my father found out about it he told me never to go underground. He said it softly but with conviction, and although it was at a time in my life when I questioned almost everything he said, after that I didn't think about becoming a miner.

What he had found that day at the bottom of the Triumph Mine did not translate well into words. It did translate into movement. Those twilit journeys across the river were a kind of dance with death in a place where the stars could shine and where the underworld was only metaphor.

My father died last fall, a month after a stroke that left him unable to speak and unable to get out of bed by himself. A blood clot after an angioplasty five years earlier had left him with half a heart. He was unable to walk more than a half-mile without becoming exhausted, but he and my mother were able to live well in Sawtooth Valley for those five years. He was able to plow the driveway in the winters and get the wood in. Every morning he would look out his window to the mountains that ring the upper end of the valley, and even if snow squalls were blowing down off the Sawtooths and the spindrifts were swirling through the outbuildings, he would say that it was wonderful to be alive for one more day.

Last summer he began to get even more frail. He had never been a big man physically, but he had weighed 140 pounds when he was a miner. His weight dropped to 115. I had a sense that his blood thinners, his beta-blockers, his cholesterol regulators, and the vitamins my mother fed him every morning were providing him with a level place to stand, but it was a place that was getting smaller and smaller.

He died trapped in his body, with a feeding tube in his stomach. During that last hellish month, his mind was intact. He understood conversation and he recognized friends, and when they told stories around his hospital bed he knew when to nod and when to smile. He tried to work with the physical therapists. He followed their instructions and worked as hard as he could to complete their exercises. After two weeks they began to look at him differently because he wasn't getting any better. My mother, brother, and I had a meeting with his rehabilitation team and when they suggested that he needed to be transferred to another facility, we had to tell them that we didn't want him moved until the date they had originally set for his discharge. It had been a date of hope. If he had showed the hoped-for improvement, it was the date he could have gone home.

He must have understood the similarities between the end of his life and the end of the lives of the thousands of animals he found waiting for him when he checked his traplines. He must have understood the quality of their waiting and understood the ones that died before he got there, thrown into lethal shock by small bones broken in leg or paw. He must have also understood that when you are eighty-three, with half a heart and a pontine stroke and no hope of dancing again, that living is a voluntary thing and that dying is a decision not to volunteer that day.

He died at three in the morning of the day after his doctors had tested his ability to swallow. They had put a solution containing barium in his mouth, and watched an X-ray movie of his tongue and throat as he tried and failed to move the barium down his esophagus. If he couldn't swallow, he couldn't go home, and he knew that. He died the day my mother was going to tour nursing homes to find a place for him to stay.

He weighed 107 pounds when he died. He was mostly bone. The X-ray photos from the swallowing test revealed that long ago he had broken his neck in two places, probably from a rockburst that had struck him when he worked in the Triumph Mine. There was a small healed displacement of the spinal column. There must have been weeks when he went to work when a stumble into a mine timber, or a sudden twist of muscle, or even raising his head to the stars would have snapped wide those broken vertebrae, killing him or leaving him a quadriplegic.

I found among his papers a living will that specified that no measures were to be taken to extend his life if he couldn't feed himself. The feeding tube had been against his wishes.

My mother stayed by his bed every day of that last month, and she talked to him about waking up to see the sun hit the peaks at the head of the valley. It kept him alive, and at that time I suppose he remembered those tough old coyotes and foxes and beaver that showed up in his traps with three legs, having chewed one of them off to get out of a trap years before. It's a distant connection, but he couldn't do much during that last month except make connections, and I suspect he made that one and that it was also one of the things that kept him alive.

It's spring. I go out to my parents' garage and the antlers still hang there, over my father's welding equipment. I never learned to use that equipment very well, and I'm having to learn. I'm going to have to go to school to do it, and as usual I'll find myself the one old guy in a class of eighteen-year-olds. This time I won't be the professor, though, and I'm terrified of screwing up. I've already planned the lie I'll tell my classmates, which is that I'm going to be a sculptor. I figure if

I'm a good enough liar, and if I practice and learn to weld well enough, the metal will flow beneath my hands and bright shapes will come out of the dark places in me that told the lie in the first place.

So I stand under the antlers and touch the cold bulk of his arc welder and the oxygen and acetylene tanks. I try on my father's welding hood and note that my head is bigger than his was. I plug in the rotary grinder that he used to burnish his welds, grasp its handles, and pull its trigger and my wrists jerk as it twists hard in my hands. I touch the anvil he used to shape heated steel and briefly lift its 130 pounds off the floor, remembering the times that he lifted it into the back of his Jeep when he made house calls. I pick up cans of welding rods and fluxes and wonder if I'll be able to learn the different steels and the art of moving a molten puddle along a ragged seam of metal.

It's an awkward, shambling, aimless dance I'm doing, but it works, because after a while my father stands beside me.

"What do you want to be a welder for?" he asks.

"I'm going to be a sculptor," I say.

He looks at me skeptically. "You remember when I tried to teach you to weld?"

I nod. It was one of those things I never got very good at, and after I hit adolescence and began using his oxygen and acetylene tanks to make balloon bombs he gave up on me and told me to stay away from his welding equipment.

"You didn't have enough patience," I say.

"I wanted you to make a living more easily than I had," he says. "I wanted you to get an education. Teach. Have your summers off. Didn't want you going down in the mines."

I grin at him. "Too bad you didn't know about committee meetings."

He shrugs. It would be a dreary business trying to make him understand. He begins to fade a little and I walk over to his toolbox and begin fumbling with hammers and screwdrivers, opening the small drawers and looking through the Allen wrenches, sockets, clamps, chisels, files, hacksaw blades, and keystock.

He walks close. "I've got things to do," he says. I ask him what those things are, but he looks right through me.

"You can't keep doing this, you know," he says. "You can't just bring me back here any time you want to."

"Sure I can," I say, and I close his toolbox and turn toward the door and step out into the sun.

Late this November I walked across the river and climbed up the hillside until I sighted the small herd of elk that grazes there in the cold early mornings. I picked a cow elk out of the herd, found her rib cage in my crosshairs, and shot her. She fell to her knees, then struggled back to her feet and moved off into the trees. I tracked the blood trail for fifty yards and then spotted her standing in a small clearing. Then she fell to her knees again, then to her side, and then, as I approached, looked back over her shoulder at me and died.

I spent the next hour gutting her. A cow elk is a big animal and I had forgotten a hoist. By the time I had gotten the intestines and heart and bullet-shattered lungs and windpipe out, I was covered with blood from my fingernails to my armpits. A dense mist rose from the carcass into the cold morning air.

The body cavity held an inch-deep lake of clotting blood that had to be cleaned out before it spoiled the meat. I pulled the hind legs over a log, and scooped blood out in double handfuls until the ground around me was soaked red. I propped the rib cage open with a pine branch so the carcass would cool out properly, picked up my rifle, and began walking home. Once there, I would put a packsaddle on the horse and gather up knives, a saw, and game bags.

As I reached the brow of the hill that rises from the Salmon River, I was able to look down at my family's forty acres. The river marks its west side and the highway its east side. The fence lines north and south are marked by crossbuck fences, and from a distance they look like markings on an old map. There, in that valley, at that moment, the place itself looked as though it had been drawn onto a photograph—as though its existence was only an inked-in one. And yet that ink—those marks, those lines—were what made it habitable, what made it human, what made it home.

I stood in and saw from the great wild for a moment, but then that vision faded leaving only the solid single horse in the pasture, the houses and the outbuildings, the Xs of the crossbucks, the smoke from the chimneys, and the pickups of other hunters moving slowly on the highway. These are not things wild animals attend to, but they are the things that make up our world. That world holds us fast, and I'm not always sure it is worth the brutal surgeries one has to perform to escape it even for a moment.

So I walked down the hill to the river, watching the pasture get closer. Then a thought: This is where I will always live. And then its dark corollary: This is where I will die. And then one small and wild hope: Someday the coyotes might let me out of this trap.

Reversing Entropy

ON A SAGEBRUSH FLAT below my family's place on the Salmon River is what remains of the dump created by Harry R. Pearce, the young man who homesteaded our place in 1928. Riveted to a rusted-out milk can in that dump is a brass tag that reads

H. R. PEARCE
TERRETON, IDAHO

Terreton is a tiny agricultural community close to Mud Lake, a shallow, weed-infested silt-bottomed lake an hour downwind from the Idaho National Environmental Engineering Laboratory, the most recent name of the National Reactor Testing Station. Radioactive waste is stored at the NRTS and always will be, at least if *always* is measured in human terms. For a couple of decades, liquid radioactive waste was injected into deep wells there, contaminating the aquifer that feeds the Thousand Springs area of the Snake River for the next twenty millennia.

Mud Lake is where my brother, working with a research team taking core samples of the lake-bottom silt, found that the yearly deposits of cesium-137 increased gradually from 1952, when the H-bomb was invented, until 1963, when aboveground nuclear testing was banned. Then the hot cesium began decreasing at the same rate it had increased, creating a perfect bell curve and a weird kink in the sedimentary record of southeastern Idaho and maybe elsewhere. I say maybe because I don't know if the cesium is a marker for aboveground H-bomb tests or if the H-bomb tests were a marker for a cultural climate that allowed for the deliberate release of radionuclides from secret government installations in desert areas of the American West.

Mud Lake is also where a Biblical-style plague descended upon the local farmers just about the time radioactive cesium values in Mud Lake's mud were fading toward normal background radiation. It was a plague of bunnies, and millions of them crawled out of rockpiles and haystacks and ditchbanks to eat the tender shoots of just-planted sugar beets and potatoes. Alfalfa disappeared from the fields before it could be baled. The road between Terreton and Mud Lake became slick with the remains of run-over bunnies. At night, people would rise from easy chairs, walk uneasily to their front doors, and turn on their porch lights. They would look out onto countless bunny eyes glowing brightly in the shadows that pooled around trees, shrubs, and fences.

The bunnies came during the same year that Idaho's Nazis began making noises in their compound near the much more beautiful Hayden Lake, a few hundred miles to the north, but still in Idaho. That year the two stories that put Idaho in the national news were the Idaho Nazis declaring their intention to found an all-white nation in the Pacific Northwest and the Mud Lake farmers organizing a giant bunny drive. Bunny-proof fences were erected at geographic choke points, and a horde of men and boys, all equipped with clubs, formed lines and walked across miles of fields and sagebrush flats, frightening thousands, and maybe hundreds of thousands, of bunnies before them. When the bunnies hit the fences, they huddled in terror until the lines of boys and men reached them and clubbed them to death. It was a multiday orgy of bunny killing, and one item that hit the networks was that an Idaho judge, responding to an appeal from animal-rights advocates, had issued an injunction banning the practice of "bunny baseball."

But when Harry R. Pearce moved from Terreton to the Sawtooth Valley he was not fleeing rabbits or Nazis or being downwind from breeder reactors and plutonium spills and experimental releases of windborne radioactive tracers. He must have been a tenant farmer in flat and treeless Terreton, with a milk cow or two, but in Sawtooth Valley farming was impossible—the ground was coarse gravel and most summer nights were cold enough to frost. What Pearce was fleeing was mud, and flatness, and being out of work unless he worked for subsistence wages for someone else.

Even though the Great Depression would not arrive for another two years, he was a harbinger of it. All he and his wife and two children possessed when they arrived in the valley was a wagon, the goods the wagon would hold, and the two mules that pulled it. If their dream was of a new life in a new place where the sky didn't threaten to suck your soul into unbounded space while the ground held fast to your shoes, it was a dream fueled by desperation.

Harry R. Pearce was a late homesteader, and the choice parts of Sawtooth Valley had already been taken up. The eighty acres he homesteaded in 1928 were in a narrow and dry part of the valley, where the Salmon River ran through a gravel plain that grew scrub willows and sagebrush. There was grass enough for the mules in the summer, but hay had to be purchased to get them through the winter. The mules also had to be inside during the winter, when the snow was four feet deep, the temperatures would hit fifty below, and even the days would stay below zero for two weeks at a time. He built his tiny, two-mule-sized barn the same year he built his homestead cabin.

He began work in the lodgepole forests that cover the foothills of the Sawtooths. It was hard work in the days before chain saws, but he must have loved wood and the working of it, because as soon as he had enough money to start his own business, he became a carpenter and lodgepole furniture maker with his own small sawmill.

His furniture shop was a long building with a shaft running through the center of its single room. The shaft was spun by a small gasoline motor and his planers, lathes, and sanders took power from it by means of belts and pulleys. By the time my parents bought the place from him in 1953, he had built an icehouse, a wood-drying cabin, a couple of equipment sheds, a fuel shed, a sawmill building, a washhouse, a chicken house, a couple of outhouses, and a doghouse. The place looked like a small town. He was building chairs and tables for restaurants and ski lodges in Ketchum and Sun Valley and was making a living. We still have a set of chairs and a kitchen table that he built. Their legs are the un-peeled trunks of lodgepole trees. After sixty years, they are still sturdy and functional and beautiful.

But by 1953, Pearce was dying, and not dying well, of a progressive emphysema contracted from decades of breath-ing wood dust, tobacco smoke, and gasoline fumes. He had given the south forty of the eighty acres to his son-in-law, who had moved in a railroad line shack to live in. My parents bought the north forty, which held the buildings, for $4,000, in 1953. Pearce and his wife had emptied out the buildings of his tools and everything else that could be sold. They moved fifty miles downriver to Challis, where they died a few years later. I remember going with my parents to visit him once, to clear up some information on water rights. He seemed small and bent and impossibly old, but I think that he was around sixty when he died.

The summer of 1954 our family moved to Sawtooth Valley. We lived in the homestead cabin. It was nineteen by twenty feet. It held a kitchen, a living room, and two eight-by-ten-foot bedrooms. My brother and I had bunks in one of the bedrooms. There was an outhouse just outside, on the river-bank, about four feet up from the water's edge.

Almost immediately we found it too small for four people. My mother wanted a larger kitchen, so my father moved the barn, which had been built on skids, next to the homestead cabin. He wired it, put linoleum on its plank floor, Sheetrocked over the manure-stained walls, and moved in an electric stove.

The next summer he tore the shafts, belts, tables, and pulleys out of the shop building. He put in a floor and partitions and a ceiling. He built forms and poured concrete for a foundation and floors in the blacksmith shop that was next to the wood shop, and then he plumbed in a real flush toilet, a bathtub, and a hot water heater. He put in a new kitchen, with a gas stove. Over time, the homestead cabin was used for a guest cabin, and then when its floor began to rot and gaps began to appear between the logs, we stored junk in it. Where the gaps between the logs got big enough to let the snow in, we stuffed them with rags and newspapers and moved out anything that could be damaged by water. We expected it to collapse under a snowload the first time we got a big winter.

By 1970, we had torn down the sawmill and the shed that held gasoline, fuel oil, and barrels of grease. We had torn down one of the buildings that had held tools. As part of a festive family marshmallow roast, we had burned down the chicken house, and the nitrates that had soaked into its wood from decades of chicken shit made it go off like a bomb. For a while we thought it would burn down the rest of the buildings on the place.

The barn that had become a kitchen was moved yet again to a far edge of the property and served as my bedroom for most of my adolescence, until we finally gave it away to a neighbor whose sons were approaching adolescence. He trailered it back to his ranch, to a spot well away from his house. The washhouse would become my sauna.

When my parents retired in 1980, they bought a small

cedar home that had been built on one of the properties that had been condemned by the Forest Service when the bill creating the Sawtooth National Recreation Area was enacted. They moved it to where the sawmill had been. I built my own house on the south end of the forty acres.

It occurs to me now that we were homesteading Pearce's homestead. At some level, we were determined to erase or alter what he had done and replace it with our own efforts. His shop became our house. His house became our storage shed. We stored saddles, harnesses, and traps in his icehouse. My father operated the sawmill for a summer, cutting house logs for a friend, but he sold the saws and machinery as soon as he found a buyer.

We changed everything we could. We put our stamp on all of the things that Pearce had left behind, until what he had left behind became all ours. My parents outlived all the people who never quit referring to our place as the Old Pearce Place. We wrested a place from a wilderness, and it wasn't the usual Idaho wilderness of lakes and trees and mountains and sage. Instead it was the wilderness of half-realized dreams that Harry R. Pearce had sold us for $4,000.

I have driven through the flat farms around Terreton, Idaho, on my way to the mountains of Montana and Wyoming, and even now, seventy-odd years after Harry R. Pearce left, I can't believe that Idaho has a place that flat and muddy and that people still live in it. I can't believe that the federal government was still giving away land in Sawtooth Valley to anyone who would put a homestead on it in 1928. I can't believe that the whole town of Terreton didn't pick up and move there. I can't believe that my parents found the courage to borrow $4,000 in 1953, when neither of them had seen that much money in one place in their lives.

I can't believe that after I cashed out of Ketchum in 1987, I was able to build this house I sit in now, and I can't believe my parents let me build it on the only spot on the property where the foothills don't block the view of the Sawtooths to the west. My mother had dreamed that she would have a house there and that she would be able to see Mount Heyburn from her kitchen window. She gave that up for a far more urgent dream that for as long as she lived, she would be able to look out of her kitchen and see my father wheelbarrowing in the evening's wood.

I also can't believe how little I know about Harry R. Pearce, how much I have to infer about his life, and how much is mystery and will remain so. In the dump where the rusted-out milk can bears his brass-embossed name, there is broken glass—much of it broken by me, as a twelve-year-old with a .22 pistol—and also the poisonous remains of the battery packs he used for his radio, the brittle fragments of tobacco tins, an old washing machine, the shards of five-gallon stoneware crocks, hunks of cast iron, and not much else. A few square five-gallon cans have large square holes in their sides, where he used their metal for sheeting or roofing. The old washing machine has the bottom cut out of it, and I think he used it as a router table for a while, and cut the bottom out so the shavings would fall to the floor. I suspect he was a good man with a pair of metal shears. In the buildings he left, I found old engine parts, fragments of harness, worn pieces of belting, punctured oil cans, burnt bearings, and immovable pulleys. One thing I can say for certain is that he never threw anything away just because it was broken.

He left some warped and yellowed books on animal husbandry in the cabin. Here and there around the property he left the axles and wheels of wagons, and we've kept these and oiled them and the wheels still turn on their axles.

The only personal thing I have of his is a framed V-mail form signed by his son, Raymond Pearce. It reads, "Greetings from Tokyo Bay. USS *Ancon.*" Then the signature, "Raymond Pearce." The USS *Ancon* is pictured on the water below the summit of a snow-marked Mount Fuji. Nothing is written on the back of the form, where a letter home was supposed to go, but there is a small black-and-white photo of Raymond—at least I think it's Raymond—floating loose beneath the glass. He's a smiling young white guy in a sailor's cap, drinking a beer. Stroh's.

The form has a place for a censor's stamp, but there's no censor's stamp on it. It was printed in the U.S. Government printing office in 1943, which means either that by 1943 people were assuming we would win the war with Japan and were printing up V-mail for the occasion, or we had already won it by 1943 and something else happened to cause Hiroshima and Nagasaki.

I found this V-mail in its frame in the attic of my cabin in Stanley. I don't know how it got there.

The summer I remodeled the drying shed into a guest cabin, I took the V-mail back upriver and hung it on the guest cabin wall as a curiosity, and it was only then that I made the connection between Harry and Raymond.

I don't know what happened to Raymond. My father says

he died young, soon after we bought the place from his father, but he's not sure. If Raymond is still alive now he's an old man. I would like to talk to him and ask him about Harry R. Pearce and if the R. stands for Raymond, and about Tokyo Bay, and if he was anywhere close when they burned down Hiroshima and Nagasaki.

I'm told that by the age of fifty you get the face you deserve, and I understand, when I look in the mirror, that this means that I have sinned less than Keith Richards.

Another aspect of being fifty, if you're me, is that you can look at photos from twenty and thirty years ago with you in them, and you can't make a direct connection to the person you were. You have to infer that person, just as you have to infer Harry R. Pearce from an old milk can, broken wagon parts, a set of chairs, and a table. Every bit of evidence is subject to disputed interpretation. The past continuously becomes estranged from the present. If I ever put this sentiment on a bumper sticker for the SUV I swore I'd never own, I'll stick it on the front bumper, and it will read, "There is no continuity of the self through time."

Which is probably putting it a little too strongly.

Because my fifty-year-old self does have a distant memory of my four-year-old self sitting in the gravel in front of Pearce's homestead cabin.

"What are you doing?" my thirty-six-year-old father asks me.

"Playing in the dirt," my four-year-old self answers. And I realize that the reason I've remembered such a trivial bit of dialogue for forty-six years is that the dirt in front of the homestead cabin is something I've walked on and played in and loved ever since the day I first touched it. It's a patch of gravel and sand, too porous to grow grass even if grass could survive the cars that have driven over it, the horses that have ground their hooves into it while being shod, and the cleats of the rubber boots of my father's fishing clients as they posed in front of the cabin with their day's catch of Chinook salmon. It's just an ordinary gravel patch, but even now I can feel the touch of it on my palm, smell its hot sunlit smell, see its textured rock and sand and small sprouts of weed and broken bits of wood. I suppose the ideal bumper sticker for the back bumper of the SUV I swore I'd never own would be, "But there is continuity of love through time."

My friend Sean Petersen has not worked as a gourmet chef since his climbing accident five years ago. He can no longer remember long strings of orders, or cook a dozen meals at once, or recognize individual voices above the general shouting that goes on in a restaurant kitchen. Sometimes he works now, but not at a steady job, and often he works for friends and works for free. His brain takes unscheduled days off that make it hard for him to stick to anybody else's schedule, and that makes it hard for him to charge for his labor.

That said, it's always a lucky night when he shows up on my doorstep offering to cook dinner. It's a good day when I've got fence to build or a roof to fix and he shows up with his tools. He has relearned how to walk and how to ski, and he's still working on relearning the guitar, and few people who meet him now have any idea that he's ever had a brain injury unless he has to keep to a schedule. There are times I envy him for his brain that takes days off, but he says it isn't as pleasant as it might look from the outside.

Sean needed a place to live. I had a sabbatical year. We decided to restore Pearce's homestead cabin so Sean could live there.

It took us four days to clean it out. A nineteen-by-twenty cabin doesn't seem large, but by the time we had pulled out bundles of traps, old packsaddles, a dead table saw, couches that had seen the birth of many generations of mice, a couple of woodstoves, military surplus photo equipment, logging chains, old pots and pans, unstuffed and overstuffed chairs, broken glass, broken tables, broken toys, broken beds, broken fishing poles, the lids to broken casseroles, tires worn through to their white nylon cords, broken radios, and a window-mount air conditioner, unused since my brother bought it back in 1971 from an airbase in Thailand, it seemed larger. It took us another half day to pull out all the nails from the walls and ceiling joists where things had been hanging.

Then we went in with a shop vacuum and sucked the dirt and mouse turds and rotten wood and bits of decayed cloth off the floor and vacuumed the walls. The attic had been insulated with flattened cardboard boxes, and it took us half a day to remove them and suck seventy years' worth of pine pollen and dust off the rafters and the ceiling. We began piling the debris in a burning pile, because I had read a pamphlet on respiratory hantavirus, and had been frightened enough by the information to buy respirators and enough vacuum hose to keep the shop vac out in the open air.

When the cabin was cleaned out, we began to rip up the floor. It had rotted through in spots, but it was in better shape than we expected. Pearce had packed in granite rocks to put the cabin on, and each lodgepole floor stringer was held six inches above the gravel by rocks. Some of the lodgepoles looked as though they had been cut last summer, having mummified perfectly in the dry darkness below the cabin floor.

When we finished pulling the floorboards out, we discovered why the cabin hadn't collapsed under the snows of seventy winters. The interior walls were bearing walls, and their uprights sat solid on flat rocks and butted into the roof structure above. The roof structure had all the braces and cross members of a much larger building, so the interior walls held up a roof that could hold four feet of snow, even if the exterior walls hadn't been there. Pearce had overengineered the whole thing.

The gaps in the walls that made the cabin look as though it was about to collapse had been caused when the bottom logs had rotted away. Some of the logs remained attached to the roof and some sagged lower. The walls looked in far worse shape than they were.

When we began to jack up the walls, the gaps disappeared. It took us a couple of days to raise the entire cabin six inches off the foundation stones. Then we went around the cabin with a chain saw and removed the bottom two logs where they hadn't rotted away altogether.

I packed fifteen wheelbarrow loads of foundation stones out from under the cabin walls. Then I shoveled three inches of gravel out of the floor. It was a dangerous job, because Pearce, I discovered, had been in the habit of sliding his used razor blades through cracks in the floorboards to get rid of them. The gravel and the razor blades amounted to thirty more wheelbarrows, and I added tetanus and septicemia to the hantavirus threat.

We borrowed Redfish Lake Lodge's cement mixer and made our own concrete, which is possible, if not easy, when you live on a giant gravel bar. We poured an exterior foundation and replaced the bottom two logs. When we let the cabin back down onto the foundation, it began to look as though it might be livable one day.

By the time we were done that November, we had put in thermal piping for a heated concrete floor, reframed and reglazed the windows, replaced every rotten log, rechinked the exterior walls, insulated the ceiling with fiberglass, built a new front door, put in new kitchen cabinets and refrigerator, patched and sealed the tin-can shingles of the roof, put in beds and a good woodstove, built a kitchen table out of the old floorboards, mounted the old pitcher pump so it spilled into a refurbished sink, and hooked it to a sixty-gallon water storage tank that sat out of sight behind a corner cabinet. We installed a restaurant-grade gas stove under a steel hood. Sean moved in his guitars and framed photographs and the framed menus of restaurants where he had been chef. He had a place to live.

The restoration of Harry R. Pearce's homestead cabin should have restored me, but it didn't.

Sean and I had tried to bring the cabin back to its original condition. But when we had replaced the floor with concrete, we had torn out a feature that made the cabin unique. Between each interior wall and the floor, Pearce had nailed in a row of flattened coffee cans and had hammered a gentle curve into them so that the floors were coved into the walls. It meant, in a practical sense, that the floors were easy to clean because there was no sharp break between floor and wall. Dust wouldn't get caught in the corners because it was all curves down there.

As I was ripping out Pearce's meticulous and intricate and rusting metalwork with a wrecking bar, I was struck by the thought that this house, with its rotten floor and sagging walls, had once been a dream house. It had been brought into existence by a man who cared how well he did things, who had a love for the moment when two perfectly cut pieces of wood fit together, who delighted in taking discarded oil cans from a dump and hammering them into beautiful, functional shapes. The roof of the cabin, those old flattened cans, is shingled so well that it still sheds water, and I found that when I went to patch the places that had rusted through, I could go to the same dump Pearce had and cut the side out of one of the cans that he hadn't cut the side out of, and patch it perfectly if I took enough time and care to loosen the nails without tearing the metal.

There on the roof I began to dream of who he was, and of the hard work behind his life, and of how he had made something out of nothing. I began to see, also, how bitter it must have been for him to realize that his emphysema would make the altitude and working in the timber and sawdust an impossible combination. I began to imagine what it must have been like to lose a son about the same time he lost his place. I began to understand why he didn't last long once he got to Challis. There on the roof I got closer to Harry R. Pearce than I am to many of the people I've known well.

It was about this time in the project that Sean began referring to the cabin as his. His friends would come by and he would show them where his kitchen would go, and his bed, and how the place would be his monastery. I kept having to remind myself that we were not restoring the cabin for me.

But after about a week of being in a bad temper every time Sean called something his that I had always thought of as mine, the thought finally became conscious: as it had for Harry R. Pearce, the time would come for me that I would lose this place, this gravel patch, the sound of this river, the clarity of this air, the brightness of this sunlight that hits this house where I write these words.

My father used to tell a story that was told to him when he was a young man by a man who, if my arithmetic is right, was as old then as my father was when he died.

"We were trying to farm on the banks of the Snake River," the old man said. "The weather hadn't been good that summer and we weren't very good farmers anyway, and by fall we didn't have a lot of food to get us through the winter. My brother and I were sent out to the river to catch fish. We figured that if we caught a sturgeon we could cut it up and can it in fruit jars and get through the winter that way, but we weren't very good fishermen either, so we didn't have a whole lot of hope. We did have a small rowboat that we'd built out of planks, so we got in it with half-a-dozen sticks of dynamite bundled together. We put a cap and a five-minute fuse on it. We rowed out to the center of the river, lit the fuse, and tossed it all overboard. We let the boat drift downstream so when the dynamited fish rose to the surface, we could just gather them up.

"It had been about five minutes when I noticed a string of little bubbles coming to the surface beside the boat. Each bubble, when it popped, would let loose a little puff of white smoke, and sure enough, when I looked down, I could see the bundle of dynamite rolling along the bottom under us, making a roll, then stopping, then making another roll and a tumble, then stopping, then rolling, all the time keeping perfect pace with the boat.

"I grabbed the oars and gave one big pull on them to get us out of there, and then the dynamite went off.

"You know," the old man told my father, "we never did find that boat."

He didn't say if his brother made it to shore, or how they ate that winter, or what it was like to live in a world where the rivers were full of fish. That world is gone now, and so is the old man who told the story. If it has a moral, I can't see it, except to say that I have a theory that the Snake River sturgeon were fished and dammed and dynamited to extinction soon after white people settled and farmed the riverbanks. The fish that people are catching and calling sturgeon now are just little rainbow trout that slipped through the fence at the Hagerman hatchery and grew to twelve foot, 400-pound mutants covered with bony tumors, pustules, and river fungus after years of bottom feeding on plutonium from Thousand Springs, fertilizer and pesticide-laden runoff from southern Idaho farms, and the periodic overflows from the Twin Falls sewage plant. They just look like sturgeon.

My thirty-eight-year-old self and I still have contact, even though it's been twelve years since he built this house I write in and eleven years since he wrote an essay, "On Going Back to Sawtooth Valley," about a world I no longer live in. He wrote about how industrial tourism had reduced the Sawtooth Valley to a museum and life to predictable ritual and how that had resulted in a loss of wonder for him.

But I know now that there's no lack of wonder in Sawtooth Valley or anywhere else. I know that ritual is the one predictable thing in a world where time's arrow leads one way, toward greater and greater disorder. I now realize that much of his life, including the writing of that essay, had been one ritual or another.

It's also been eleven years since he left Sawtooth Valley. Even though he had the skills to make a living as a writer and carpenter and cement worker there, and even though he loved the place, he chose instead to take a one-year visiting professorship at Albertson

College of Idaho in Caldwell. Caldwell is western Idaho's version of Mud Lake.

Caldwell is where I teach English Composition and make mortgage payments on a house and car payments on the SUV that I swore I'd never own with the Canyon County plates I swore I'd never have. It's where I meet my financial adviser so I can retire in fifteen years and move back for more than just summers to the place I love more than anyplace else, the place my thirty-eight-year-old self left.

Of course I won't be me when I retire. I'll be someone else. I hope that old guy loves the same things I do. I hope he's got his wits about him and that he thinks about me once in a while. I hope he doesn't think I'm an idiot. I hope he'll appreciate all I've done for him, the pathetic old bastard.

When I told my father I had been a teacher long enough to earn a sabbatical year, he looked at me and said, "They just give you a year off."

There might have been reproach in his voice, or it might have been that I'd heard reproach in other voices asking the same question.

"The problem," I said, "is that they expect me to improve myself."

It's true. Institutions seldom grant anyone free time. They expect you to use a summer or a sabbatical to reverse your headlong slide into entropy. You'll write an epic. Sculpt a piece of granite. Photograph the ten-billion-year-old light of a galaxy and pretend its stars still exist. Travel. Learn a new software. Learn Arabic. Rejuvenate your teaching.

Add to your self.

It's a model of self that we use in education and in retirement planning and in obituaries. The self is seen as a kind of dump truck, filled over a lifetime with places and relationships and diplo-

*mas and money. At death, the whole load gets emptied out, pref-
erably at the feet of a deity who approves of having stuff and keeping it.*

*But there's another model of self out there, one that fits better,
one that is drifting slowly away from the National Reactor Testing
Station, out into the eons-old aquifer under the bunny-infested
sagebrush of eastern Idaho: the self as radioactive isotope, glowing
in the Pleistocene darkness, decaying into daughter isotopes that in
turn decay into their daughters, moving by half-lives toward death
but never getting there as long as there's an alpha particle to be cast
off. If there was anything stable behind that glow there wouldn't be
a glow to see. What we can hope for is to glow brightly in the moment of our decay, to remember the brightness of others, and to feel
the faint heat that remains in the things they touched.*

ABOUT THE AUTHOR

John Rember was born in Sun Valley, Idaho, and raised in the nearby Sawtooth Valley. He was educated at Harvard and the University of Montana. He teaches English at Albertson College in Caldwell, Idaho, and is the author of two previous books, *Coyote in the Mountains* and *Cheerleaders from Gomorrah*.